Weight Watchers®

Slim Ways™

MEXICAN

Macmillan • USA

WEIGHT WATCHERS

Since 1963, Weight Watchers has grown from a handful of members to a leading name in safe, sensible weight control. Today millions enjoy our popular, expanding line of convenience foods, best-selling cookbooks, audio and video tapes and weight-loss management products.

For best weight loss results, we recommend that you attend Weight Watchers meetings, follow the Weight Watchers food plan and participate in a regular program of physical activity. For the Weight Watchers meeting nearest you, call 1-800-651-6000.

We would like to acknowledge the enthusiasm, patience and dedication of our team as they worked their way through the cuisines of Mexico to bring you this collection of recipes—Recipe Developers: Luisa Gray, Tamara Holt, Toni Oppenheimer; Recipe Editor: Patricia Barnett; Nutrition Consultant: Lynne S. Hill, M.S., R.D., L.D.—and the inspiration provided by the fine Mexican cooking and writing of Deann and Rick Bayless and Dianne Kennedy.

Cover photo by Martin Jacobs

Cover photo: Beef and Potato Tacos, page 63

SKU: 359 6102

MACMILLAN

A Simon & Schuster Company
1633 Broadway
New York, NY 10019-6785

Macmillan is a registered trademark of Macmillan, Inc.
WEIGHT WATCHERS and SLIM WAYS are registered trademarks of Weight Watchers International, Inc.

Library of Congress Cataloging-in-Publication Data

Weight Watchers slim ways : Mexican.
      p.   cm.
   Includes index.
   ISBN 0-02-860384-2 (alk. paper)
   1. Low-fat diet—Recipes.   2. Cookery, Mexican.   I. Weight
Watchers International.
   RM237.7.W44   1996
   641.5'638—dc20   95-18545
                        CIP
Manufactured in the United States of America
10 9 8 7 6 5 4 3 2 1

CONTENTS

INTRODUCTION

Based on corn and chile peppers, today's Mexican food is an amalgam of the foods of the indigenous Mayans and Aztecs with those of Renaissance Spain, along with the Moorish influences that are also a part of the Spanish culture. When the Spaniards first arrived in Mexico, they found a sophisticated society with markets that sold hundreds of varieties of chile peppers, as well as fruits and other vegetables. And there was corn—white, yellow, red and blue— permeating all aspects of the culture.

Mexican food is *not* fast food, though some of the recipes in this book are quickly prepared. Techniques, as much as ingredients, are key to producing the unique quality of this ancient cuisine. These techniques are somewhat different from European-style methods but, with a little practice, they will become second nature. Mexican food is especially well suited to low-fat, low-calorie cooking. The intense flavors produced by the combinations of ingredients and techniques make the food so delicious and satisfying that you don't feel deprived.

EQUIPMENT

Tortilla press: You can get good tortillas in ethnic markets, in some supermarkets (especially in the southwestern United States and in Mexican neighborhoods of large cities) or by mail (see Sources, page x). But if you want to make your own, a press is an inexpensive convenience. You can sometimes find presses in ethnic markets, or mail-order catalogs. Avoid the self-heating tortilla makers; you can't control the heat, and the nonstick surface is so slippery that the tortilla is inclined to squirt out of the machine.

Zester: Many recipes call for citrus zest, the very thin outermost peel of limes, lemons, oranges and grapefruits. You want to avoid the pith, the bitter white membrane just beneath the zest, so a zester, which looks rather like a perforated bottle opener, is very useful. If you can't find a zester, use the side of a vegetable grater to make grated zest, or try a vegetable peeler to make long, thin strips.

INGREDIENTS

CHILE PEPPERS

Chile peppers come in dozens of varieties and degrees of heat. They are, along with corn, the basis of Mexican cooking. Rich in vitamins and low in calories, they provide vivid flavor as well as heat. The skin of the chile pepper has a natural gloss and may sport any color from apple green to nearly black, including red, orange, yellow and every shade in between. The heat is caused by a chemical known as capsaicin, which is so potent that it is used in defensive "pepper spray" and in medicinal ointments to counteract the pain of arthritis and shingles. You can defuse the heat of a chile pepper somewhat by removing the veins and seeds, but the chile's heat varies tremendously, even from one end of a plant to the other. To soothe a mouth overheated by an unexpectedly fierce chile pepper, drink milk, eat some yogurt or ice cream, or eat a spoonful of sugar.

For directions on roasting and peeling fresh chile peppers, see Techniques, page ix.

FRESH CHILE PEPPERS

Caution: Chiles are potent, so if you are handling hot chile peppers, wear surgical gloves (which cost just a few cents a pair in drugstores) and do not touch your eyes (or any other tender or moist parts of your body) without first washing your hands thoroughly.

With so many varieties available, there is enough room in this book for descriptions of only a few of the most popular ones.

Habanero: The hottest and most delicious chile pepper of all, habanero is walnut shaped and apricot colored, with a fruity scent. It can be used raw or cooked and should be treated with respect; be sure to wear gloves when handling it!

Hungarian wax: Long, yellow or orange-red, it is medium-hot and great for pickling or using raw in salads.

Jalapeño: Probably the most popular chile pepper in the United States, this tapered pepper (deep green when unripe and red when ripe) is delicious raw in salsas and as a garnish, pickled or roasted and peeled in cooked dishes.

Mulato: This pepper is brownish black and mild, with a sweet, chocolatey flavor. It is used only in cooked sauces, such as Molé Poblano (see page 156).

Poblano: This is perhaps the most useful chile pepper. Shaped like an elongated bell pepper (but infinitely more flavorful), it is generally used roasted and peeled. You can slice them, dice them or stuff them; look for the smoothest peppers to make peeling easier.

Serrano: This slim chile pepper packs quite a wallop! Either green or bright red, it is really too small to peel and is usually used whole. You can seed and devein it if you want a slightly less incendiary flavor. Grilled with barbecued meats, sliced into salads and salsas or tossed with a seafood sauté, serrano peppers give food an exciting punch.

DRIED CHILE PEPPERS

If you think about the difference in taste between a grape and a raisin, you will understand why dried, or dried and smoked, chile peppers add so much to the variety and complexity of Mexican flavors. Dried chile peppers should be free from mold and somewhat flexible. Store them in a closed plastic bag at room temperature; they will keep almost indefinitely. Here are descriptions of a few.

Ancho: This is the dried form of the poblano pepper. With an almost meaty flavor, it can be stuffed, or chopped and used in sauces.

Chile de Arbol: This is a hot one! About three inches long, slender and reddish in color, it is used in sauces and stews. There is no need to soak it after toasting; just grind it along with the other spices in the recipe.

Chipotle: The dried, smoked version of jalapeño, it is dark brown and leathery. Do not remove seeds and veins; the entire pepper can be pickled or added to soups, sauces and stews for a smoky heat. The canned version, chipotle peppers in adobo sauce, is packed in a dark, richly flavored sauce. For convenience, purée the peppers and sauce in a food processor or blender and refrigerate in a covered container. A spoonful or two (it's *picante*, so be careful) turns a plain dish, or even a commercial soup or sauce, into something fragrant and delicious.

Guajillo: About five inches long and quite thin, this pepper is medium hot and has a tough skin and sharp flavor that is delicious in cooked sauces and stews. Even after pureeing the peppers, some recipes require that the skin be strained out of a sauce before serving.

Pasilla: This pepper is about six inches long by three-quarters of an inch wide, blackish in color, mild and fragrant. It is used in sauces and as a condiment.

MEXICAN CHEESES

You may find authentic Mexican cheeses in your local market; if not, use soft-textured farmer cheese or feta cheese that you have soaked for an hour in cold water and drained. Monterey Jack, often called for in Mexican recipes, is widely available in most areas, so do try it in recipes that call for this variety of hard cheese. Although the extra-sharp variety of cheddar cheese is not authentically Mexican, the stronger flavor works well when using small amounts. A little Parmesan cheese will boost the flavor of other cheeses.

SEEDS AND NUTS

Achiote or annatto seeds: These very hard, red seeds, used in seasoning pastes, are widely available. Grind them in an electric spice mill, the mini-jar attachment on a blender, a mortar and pestle or an electric coffee grinder.

Sesame seeds, pumpkin seeds, aniseeds and almonds: These high-fat ingredients are generally used as flavorings. Toasted, they add depth, richness and color to sauces, soups and stews, and because they are used in such small quantities they supply only a small amount of calories and fat.

FRUITS AND VEGETABLES

Chayote: Similar in size and shape to a pear, this squash-like vegetable has a pleasant, mild flavor. Remove the skin with a vegetable peeler or sharp knife, and slice or dice the pulp before using. The seed is edible and can be sliced and added to the dish for a delicate, nutty flavor.

Jicama: Although unattractive before paring, this slightly sweet, nutty-tasting tuber is widely available and can be eaten raw or cooked. Once pared, its creamy white color, flavor and crunchy texture are similar to a water chestnut. Buy the smallest one you can find; one jicama goes a long way. To use, cut it into sections and remove the skin and fibers under the skin with a sharp paring knife. Jicama stays crisp even when cooked and absorbs flavors readily; use it in salads, in raw salsas and in soups for a pleasant crunch.

Plantain: This relative of the banana, which is *always* eaten cooked, is amazingly versatile. When pale green in color, it is starchy and can be used like a potato in soups and stews. When yellow-ripe, it can be cooked and mashed, grilled or sauteed and served as a vegetable. When black-ripe, it can be used as a side dish, baked like a sweet potato, peeled and cooked in a sauce or made into a dessert. Although it will hold its shape and absorb flavors much better than a banana, the skin usually won't "zip" off like the peel of a banana. Use a sharp knife to cut it into thirds, then cut along the ridges of the skin. Pull the skin off along these cuts and trim off any brown, woody areas before using.

Tomatillo: A cousin of the gooseberry, it is hard and pale green, with a papery husk and is a typical component of many sauces, soups, salsas and stews. It adds a tart, unique flavor and is widely available fresh or canned.

Corn Products

Masa harina: This is parched corn treated with lime and ground. Quaker makes an acceptable version. This is necessary for tortillas, but for all other recipes you may substitute corn meal. If the corn meal is a major ingredient, use stone ground (available in health food stores), which has more flavor.

Techniques

To brine shrimp: This simple process improves even mediocre shrimp in the shell; it does *not* make them salty but gives them a fresh taste and texture that is well worth the small amount of work. Combine ¹/₂ cup coarse (kosher) salt with 1 cup boiling water; stir to dissolve thoroughly. Add 3 cups cold water, then the shrimp; let stand 45 minutes. Drain; rinse thoroughly with cold water.

To roast tomatoes: Use firm, ripe tomatoes. Core tomatoes; cut into halves. Preheat broiler. Line baking sheet or pie pan with foil; set tomato halves, cut-side down, onto prepared baking sheet. Broil tomatoes 4–6" from heat until skin is blistered and lightly charred. Turn tomatoes over; broil until cut side is lightly charred.

To roast garlic: Use large, unpeeled cloves of garlic. Preheat broiler. Line baking sheet or pie pan with foil; set garlic cloves onto prepared baking sheet. Broil garlic 4–6" from heat until skin is dark brown. Turn garlic over; broil until other side is dark brown. Cool, then peel.

To roast onions: Preheat broiler. Line baking sheet or pie pan with foil; set unpeeled onions onto prepared baking sheet. Broil, 8" from heat, turning frequently with tongs, until skin is evenly charred on all sides. Cool, then peel.

To roast tomatillos: Remove and discard husks from tomatillos; wash tomatillos thoroughly in cool water to remove sticky coating. Preheat broiler. Line baking sheet or pie pan with foil; set tomatillos onto prepared baking sheet. Broil tomatillos 4–6" from heat until skin is lightly charred. Turn tomatillos over; broil until other side is lightly charred.

To roast fresh chile peppers: Preheat broiler. Line baking sheet or pie pan with foil; set whole peppers onto prepared baking sheet. Broil peppers 4–6" from heat, turning frequently with tongs, until skin is lightly charred on all sides. Transfer peppers to bowl; let cool. Wearing surgical gloves, peel, seed and devein peppers over bowl to catch juices. (This technique works well for bell peppers as well, but because they're not hot the gloves are not necessary.)

To prepare dried chile peppers: Break or cut off pepper stems. With sharp knife or gloved hands, split peppers; remove seeds if instructed to do so in the recipe. Some recipes call for the split peppers to be toasted in a nonstick skillet, either dry or with a little oil, then soaked in very hot water for 10–20 minutes. If peppers tend to "float," weigh them down with a small plate to keep them submerged. They are then pureed in a blender or food processor, usually with tomatoes or some liquid. Sometimes this purée is strained to improve the texture and appearance of the finished dish.

To fry sauce: In addition to roasting or toasting, Mexican cooks add and concentrate flavor by frying sauces. To fry sauce, in a nonstick skillet, cook pureed ingredients with a little oil over high heat, stirring constantly, until very thick.

To grind seeds, herbs and spices: Seasoning pastes and spice mixtures are characteristic of Mexican cookery. The mini-jar attachment on a blender, an electric spice mill or an electric coffee grinder, used only for spices, are the best tools for this. Or you can, of course, use a mortar and pestle. Be sure to clean whatever device you use by wiping it with a damp paper towel after grinding to avoid the buildup of oils, which may turn rancid.

To prepare corn husks for tamales: Tamales can be made in foil packets, but corn husks add a lovely flavor and also look pretty. Don't be intimidated; it's not difficult! Husks are available dried (see Sources, page x), or you can use fresh husks, which always seem to be smaller. To use dried husks, soak them in simmering water for ten minutes; remove from heat. Let stand, covered, 1–2 hours, until pliable. Husks should be at least six inches across at the wide end; you can overlap two husks if necessary. Place about 2 tablespoons of tamale mixture on center of each husk; fold long sides over filling to enclose. With kitchen string, tie both ends closed, leaving room for filling to expand. (If desired, you can fold one or both ends over filling rather than tying ends closed.) Most tamales take about 1 1/2 hours to steam. Fill large saucepan with one inch of water; bring water to a simmer. Line steamer basket with a few extra corn husks, leaving some gaps between them. Place tamales in prepared steamer basket; cover with a few more husks and a clean tea towel. Steam, tightly covered, adding boiling water to saucepan as needed.

To prepare fresh corn: If a recipe calls for fresh corn kernels, remove kernels from cob by first removing husk and silk. Holding ear of corn vertically in one hand, rest one end on a cutting board; with a sharp knife, slice lengthwise along ear to remove kernels (do not cut into cob). Transfer kernels to a bowl. If recipe says to reserve corn juices, while holding cob over bowl, scrape cob with a spoon to extract juices; these juices add flavor and help to thicken soups and stews. If fresh corn is unavailable, frozen corn kernels make a suitable substitute.

Canned beans: We recommend draining and rinsing canned beans in order to remove excess sodium.

Sources

Most of the ingredients in the recipes in this book are widely available. For those that are not, here are a couple of mail-order sources:

> The CMC Company
> P.O. Box 322
> Avalon, New Jersey 08202
> Phone: 1-800-CMC-2780

> Foods of All Nations
> 2121 Ivy Road
> Charlottesville, Virginia 22903
> Phone: 1-800-368-3998

In addition, investigate ethnic markets and gourmet stores. If there is a large Mexican population in your city, many supermarkets will carry characteristic produce and groceries.

APPETIZERS
AND DIPS

WHITE BEAN-CILANTRO DIP

Makes 4 servings

1 pound drained cooked white
  kidney (cannellini) beans
3 ounces yogurt cheese*
2 tablespoons fresh lime juice
1 garlic clove, crushed

$^1/_4$ teaspoon mild or hot chili
  powder
$^1/_4$ teaspoon salt
$^1/_2$ cup finely chopped fresh
  cilantro

In food processor, combine beans, yogurt cheese, juice, garlic, chili powder and salt; with on-off motion, pulse processor several times until mixture is combined but still lumpy. Add cilantro; with on-off motion, pulse processor just until combined (do not purée). Transfer mixture to serving bowl; refrigerate until chilled.

Each serving ($^1/_3$ cup) provides: 2 Proteins, 15 Optional Calories

Per serving: 163 Calories, 1 g Total Fat, 0 g Saturated Fat, 0 mg Cholesterol, 155 mg Sodium, 29 g Total Carbohydrate, 4 g Dietary Fiber, 12 g Protein, 89 mg Calcium

  * *To prepare yogurt cheese, line a colander with cheesecloth; place in deep bowl. Spoon 3/4 cup plain nonfat yogurt (without gelatin or other additives) into colander; refrigerate, covered, at least 5 hours or overnight. Discard accumulated liquid. Makes about 3 ounces.*

QUICK BEAN DIP

Makes 8 servings

1 pound drained cooked black
  beans
$^1/_4$ cup mild or hot salsa

1 tablespoon red wine vinegar
$^1/_2$ teaspoon dried oregano leaves

In food processor, combine beans, salsa, vinegar and oregano; purée until smooth.

Each serving ($^1/_4$ cup + 1 tablespoon) provides: $^1/_4$ Vegetable, 1 Protein

Per serving: 78 Calories, 0 g Total Fat, 0 g Saturated Fat, 0 mg Cholesterol, 81 mg Sodium, 14 g Total Carbohydrate, 1 g Dietary Fiber, 5 g Protein, 17 mg Calcium

TOMATO-CHIPOTLE PEPPER DIP

Serve this rich, hot dip with tortilla chips when friends come over. Serving a large group? Just multiply the recipe to fit.

Makes 4 servings

2 teaspoons vegetable oil
$^3/_4$ cup chopped onions
1 medium dried chipotle pepper, seeded and chopped
1 garlic clove, minced
$^1/_2$ teaspoon ground cumin
1 medium red bell pepper, roasted, peeled and seeded (see page ix for roasting technique)

$^1/_3$ cup + 2 teaspoons tomato paste
2 tablespoons nonfat sour cream
1 tablespoon distilled white vinegar
$^1/_2$ teaspoon salt

1. In large nonstick skillet, heat oil; add onions, chipotle pepper, garlic and cumin. Cook over medium-low heat, stirring frequently, 10 minutes, until onions are tender. Add 2 tablespoons water; cook, stirring frequently, 10 minutes longer, until vegetables are golden brown.
2. Transfer onion mixture to food processor. Add bell pepper, tomato paste, sour cream, vinegar and salt; purée until smooth.

Each serving ($^1/_4$ cup) provides: $^1/_2$ Fat, 2 Vegetables, 5 Optional Calories

Per serving: 77 Calories, 3 g Total Fat, 0 g Saturated Fat, 0 mg Cholesterol, 476 mg Sodium, 12 g Total Carbohydrate, 2 g Dietary Fiber, 2 g Protein, 36 mg Calcium

TOMATILLO-VEGETABLE DIP

Tomatillos are widely available in Mexican groceries; this cousin of the gooseberry is a typical component of many sauces, soups, salsas and stews. Here, they add tartness to a wonderful vegetable dip.

Makes 4 servings

9 medium tomatillos, husked

4 large plum tomatoes, halved

2 medium red bell peppers, seeded and cut into thin strips

2 medium jalapeño peppers (see page v)

2 teaspoons vegetable oil

1 garlic clove, minced

Pinch salt

$^1/_4$ cup finely diced onion

2 tablespoons chopped fresh cilantro

1 tablespoon fresh lime juice

1. Preheat oven to 400°F.
2. In large bowl, combine tomatillos, tomatoes, bell and jalapeño peppers and oil; toss to coat.
3. Transfer tomatillo mixture to large baking pan; roast 1 hour, until tomatillos and peppers are very soft. Remove from oven; let cool until easy to handle.
4. Peel tomatillos; peel and seed peppers. Finely chop tomatillos, tomatoes and bell peppers; transfer to medium bowl. Finely mince jalapeño peppers with garlic and salt; add to bowl with tomatillos. Add onion, cilantro and juice; mix well. Serve warm or at room temperature.

Each serving ($^1/_4$ cup) provides: 3 $^3/_4$ Vegetables, 20 Optional Calories

Per serving: 110 Calories, 4 g Total Fat, 0 g Saturated Fat, 0 mg Cholesterol, 41 mg Sodium, 18 g Total Carbohydrate, 2 g Dietary Fiber, 4 g Protein, 32 mg Calcium

GUACAMOLE

This appetizer-salad, with plenty of tomatoes and onions, gets a lot of mileage out of the rich avocado. For the best flavor and texture, be sure the avocado is perfectly ripe. Serve as a salad or on a bed of lettuce with tortilla chips for dipping.

Makes 8 servings

1 ripe medium avocado, peeled, pitted and cut into quarters
2 medium tomatoes, finely diced
1 medium jalapeño or serrano pepper, seeded, deveined and minced (see page v)
1 cup minced onions
$^1/_4$ cup minced fresh cilantro
2 teaspoons fresh lime juice
$^1/_4$ teaspoon salt

1. In medium bowl, combine 1 avocado quarter, $^1/_4$ cup of the tomatoes, half the pepper, 1 tablespoon of the onions and half the cilantro; with fork, mash mixture together into a medium-coarse paste.
2. Finely dice remaining avocado quarters. Add diced avocado, the remaining tomatoes, pepper, onions and cilantro, the juice and salt to paste mixture; stir to combine.

Each serving ($^1/_2$ cup) provides: 1 Fat, 1 Vegetable

Per serving: 63 Calories, 4 g Total Fat, 1 g Saturated Fat, 0 mg Cholesterol, 76 mg Sodium, 6 g Total Carbohydrate, 1 g Dietary Fiber, 1 g Protein, 12 mg Calcium

HOT CHEESE DIP

Sometimes you just want something *gooey,* and this is it: hot, cheesy and as *picante* as you like! Serve the dip with tortilla chips or cut up raw vegetables; it also makes a fine topping for a baked potato.

Makes 4 servings

1 teaspoon corn oil
¹/₂ cup finely chopped onion
¹/₂ cup vegetable broth or
   low-sodium chicken broth
1 tablespoon cornstarch
¹/₄ teaspoon salt
Pinch ground red pepper

3 ounces extra-sharp cheddar
   cheese, shredded
1 cup finely diced plum tomatoes
1 medium jalapeño pepper,
   seeded, deveined and minced
   (see page v)

1. In medium saucepan, heat oil; add onion. Cook over medium heat, stirring frequently, 3–4 minutes, until onion is tender.
2. In small bowl, with wire whisk, combine broth, cornstarch, salt and red pepper, blending until cornstarch is dissolved. Add broth mixture to onion mixture; cook, stirring constantly, 2 minutes, until mixture begins to thicken. Reduce heat to low; simmer, stirring frequently, 5 minutes, until mixture is very thick.
3. Add cheese to broth mixture. Cook, stirring constantly, 2 minutes, until cheese is melted. Remove from heat; stir in tomatoes and jalapeño pepper; serve immediately.

Each serving (¹/₂ cup) provides: ¹/₄ Fat, 1 Vegetable, 1 Protein, 10 Optional Calories

Per serving with vegetable broth: 124 Calories, 8 g Total Fat, 5 g Saturated Fat, 22 mg Cholesterol, 397 mg Sodium, 7 g Total Carbohydrate, 1 g Dietary Fiber, 6 g Protein, 161 mg Calcium

Per serving with chicken broth: 125 Calories, 9 g Total Fat, 5 g Saturated Fat, 22 mg Cholesterol, 286 mg Sodium, 6 g Total Carbohydrate, 1 g Dietary Fiber, 6 g Protein, 163 mg Calcium

CHILE CON QUESO

This popular dip has many different forms; this one uses cream cheese for a light and creamy texture. Enjoy it with tortilla chips or vegetable dippers.

Makes 4 servings

1 teaspoon vegetable oil
$^1/_4$ cup finely chopped onion
1 cup low-fat (1%) milk
2 tablespoons all-purpose flour
$^3/_4$ cup chopped tomato
$^1/_2$ cup drained canned mild
   or hot chopped green chile
   peppers

$^1/_4$ cup light cream cheese
$^1/_4$ teaspoon salt
$^1/_4$ teaspoon freshly ground black
   pepper

1. In medium saucepan, heat oil; add onion. Cook over medium heat, stirring frequently, 3–4 minutes, until onion is tender.
2. Meanwhile, in small bowl, with wire whisk, combine milk and flour, blending until flour is dissolved. Stir milk mixture into onion mixture; cook, stirring constantly, until mixture comes to a boil. Continue to cook, stirring constantly, 5–6 minutes longer, until mixture thickens.
3. Add tomato and chile peppers to mixture; cook, stirring occasionally, 4 minutes. Stir in cheese, salt and black pepper; cook, stirring constantly, until cheese is melted. Serve warm.

Each serving ($^1/_2$ cup) provides: $^1/_4$ Milk, $^1/_4$ Fat, $^3/_4$ Vegetable, 45 Optional Calories

Per serving: 100 Calories, 5 g Total Fat, 2 g Saturated Fat, 10 mg Cholesterol, 493 mg Sodium, 10 g Total Carbohydrate, 1 g Dietary Fiber, 4 g Protein, 105 mg Calcium

SPICY POTATO CHIPS

These baked chips make great snacks; dip them into White Bean–Cilantro Dip, Quick Bean Dip (see page 2 for both recipes) or fresh salsa.

Makes 6 servings

2 teaspoons mild or hot chili
  powder
$^3/_4$ teaspoon ground cumin

$^1/_2$ teaspoon salt
15 ounces baking potatoes, pared
  and very thinly sliced

1. Preheat oven to 425°F. Spray 2 baking sheets with nonstick cooking spray.
2. In small bowl, combine chili powder, cumin and salt.
3. Arrange potato slices in a single layer on prepared baking sheets; spray lightly with nonstick cooking spray. Bake 1 batch at a time 7–10 minutes, until golden brown and crispy.
4. Transfer first batch of potatoes to large bowl. Sprinkle potatoes with half the seasoning mixture; toss to coat. Transfer coated chips to serving bowl. Repeat with remaining chips and seasoning mixture.

Each serving (1$^1/_2$ ounces) provides: $^1/_2$ Bread

Per serving: 62 Calories, 1 g Total Fat, 0 g Saturated Fat, 0 mg Cholesterol, 195 mg Sodium, 13 g Total Carbohydrate, 1 g Dietary Fiber, 2 g Protein, 11 mg Calcium

NACHOS

These are much more delicious than the greasy concoctions served in many Tex-Mex restaurants! To prepare individual servings, arrange the tortilla pieces in small shallow ramekins and divide the toppings evenly on the chips.

Makes 4 servings

Four 6" corn tortillas, each cut into eighths

3 medium poblano peppers, roasted, peeled, seeded and sliced (see page v; see page ix for roasting technique)

2 servings (1 cup) Salsa Cruda (see page 162)*

$^3/_4$ ounce sharp cheddar cheese, shredded

$^3/_4$ ounce Monterey Jack cheese, shredded

$^1/_4$ cup nonfat sour cream

$^1/_4$ cup plain nonfat yogurt

1. Preheat oven to 325°F. Spray baking sheet with nonstick cooking spray.
2. Place tortilla pieces in a single layer on baking sheet; bake 20–30 minutes, until golden and crisp.
3. Preheat broiler.
4. Arrange baked tortilla pieces, point-side out, in small flameproof baking dish; sprinkle evenly with peppers. Top tortilla mixture with Salsa Cruda, then cheddar and Monterey Jack cheeses; broil 4" from heat 3–4 minutes, until cheese is bubbling.
5. In small bowl, combine sour cream and yogurt; spoon over tortilla mixture. Serve immediately.

Each serving provides: $1^1/_2$ Vegetables, $^1/_2$ Protein, 1 Bread, 20 Optional Calories

Per serving: 144 Calories, 4 g Total Fat, 2 g Saturated Fat, 11 mg Cholesterol, 164 mg Sodium, 21 g Total Carbohydrate, 2 g Dietary Fiber, 7 g Protein, 181 mg Calcium

* If desired, 1 cup prepared salsa may be substituted for the Salsa Cruda; increase Vegetable Selections to 1 $^3/_4$.

Per serving with prepared salsa: 153 Calories, 4 g Total Fat, 2 g Saturated Fat, 11 mg Cholesterol, 766 mg Sodium, 22 g Total Carbohydrate, 2 g Dietary Fiber, 7 g Protein, 177 mg Calcium

MIXED ROASTED PEPPER SPREAD

Mexican cooking thrives on the vast variety of peppers; this spread spotlights three popular types, combining sweetness and fire in one fabulous mixture. Roasting brings out the flavor of the peppers and creates a wonderful texture as well.

Makes 4 servings

2 medium sweet Italian peppers, seeded and diced
2 medium poblano peppers, seeded and diced (see page vi)
1 medium red bell pepper, seeded and diced
4 garlic cloves, crushed

2 teaspoons olive oil
2 tablespoons chopped fresh flat-leaf parsley
1 teaspoon fresh lemon juice
$^{1}/_{4}$ teaspoon salt
$^{1}/_{4}$ teaspoon freshly ground black pepper

1. Preheat oven to 400°F.
2. In medium bowl, combine Italian, poblano and bell peppers, garlic and oil; toss to coat.
3. Transfer pepper mixture to large baking pan; roast $1^{1}/_{2}$ hours, until peppers are very soft. Remove from oven; leave oven on.
4. Add $^{1}/_{2}$ cup water to pepper mixture; stir to combine, scraping up browned bits from bottom of pan. Bake 5 minutes longer.
5. Return pepper mixture to medium bowl; stir in parsley, juice, salt and black pepper; mash with back of wooden spoon until paste forms. Serve warm or at room temperature.

Each serving ($^{1}/_{4}$ cup) provides: $^{1}/_{2}$ Fat, 2 Vegetables

Per serving: 57 Calories, 2 g Total Fat, 0 g Saturated Fat, 0 mg Cholesterol, 140 mg Sodium, 9 g Total Carbohydrate, 2 g Dietary Fiber, 1 g Protein, 21 mg Calcium

MINI CHIMICHANGAS

These little surprise packages adapt well to any filling; they are terrific as snacks or party food.

Makes 6 servings

1 tablespoon olive oil
1 cup thinly sliced onions
1 cup julienned red bell pepper
1 cup julienned zucchini
1 medium jalapeño pepper, seeded, deveined and minced (see page v)
1 garlic clove, minced
2 tablespoons red-wine vinegar
$^1/_2$ teaspoon mild or hot chili powder
$^1/_2$ teaspoon ground cumin

$^1/_2$ teaspoon salt
4 ounces skinless boneless cooked chicken breast, shredded
3 tablespoons chopped fresh flat-leaf parsley
Twelve 6" flour tortillas
3 ounces sharp cheddar cheese, finely shredded
$^1/_4$ cup egg substitute
$^1/_3$ cup + 2 teaspoons nonfat sour cream

1. Preheat oven to 400°F. Spray baking sheet with nonstick cooking spray.
2. To prepare filling, in medium nonstick skillet, heat oil; add onions. Cook over medium heat, stirring frequently, 3–4 minutes, until onions are tender. Add bell pepper, zucchini, jalapeño pepper, garlic and $^1/_4$ cup water; bring liquid to a boil. Cook over medium heat, stirring frequently, 7 minutes, until vegetables are tender. Add vinegar, chili powder, cumin and salt; cook, stirring frequently, 3 minutes longer. Stir in chicken and parsley; remove from heat.
3. Onto bottom third of each tortilla, spoon an equal amount of filling and cheese; fold tortillas envelope-fashion to enclose. Place filled tortillas, seam-side down and 2" apart, on prepared baking sheet; brush evenly with egg substitute and spray lightly with nonstick cooking spray. Bake 20 minutes, until tortillas are golden brown. Serve each filled tortilla topped with $1^1/_2$ teaspoons sour cream.

Each serving (2 chimichangas) provides: $^1/_2$ Fat, $1^1/_4$ Vegetables, $1^1/_2$ Proteins, 2 Breads, 10 Optional Calories

Per serving: 282 Calories, 12 g Total Fat, 4 g Saturated Fat, 32 mg Cholesterol, 509 mg Sodium, 28 g Total Carbohydrate, 2 g Dietary Fiber, 15 g Protein, 194 mg Calcium

STUFFED JALAPEÑO PEPPERS

This combination of slightly crunchy hot pepper and creamy filling makes a delicious hors d'oeuvre, or serve it as a side dish with vegetable soup for a special lunch.

Makes 8 servings

12 large jalapeño peppers (2$^1/_2$" long), halved lengthwise, seeded and deveined (reserve 2 teaspoons seeds) (see page v)
$^1/_2$ teaspoon cumin seeds
$^1/_2$ cup nonfat cream cheese, at room temperature

3 ounces extra-sharp cheddar cheese, grated
2 tablespoons plain dried bread crumbs
$^1/_4$ teaspoon dried oregano leaves

1. Preheat oven to 425°F. Line baking sheet with foil; spray foil with nonstick cooking spray.
2. In small nonstick skillet, toast reserved jalapeño seeds and cumin seeds over medium-low heat, stirring constantly, 2–5 minutes, until fragrant and golden; transfer to small bowl.
3. Add cream and cheddar cheeses to toasted seeds; with fork, mash mixture together until well blended.
4. Stuff each pepper half with an equal amount of cheese mixture; set aside.
5. On small plate, combine bread crumbs and oregano. Dip filled side of each pepper into bread crumb mixture; set on prepared baking sheet, crumb-side up. Bake 10 minutes, until lightly browned; serve immediately.

Each serving (3 halves) provides: 2$^1/_4$ Vegetables, $^1/_2$ Protein, 25 Optional Calories

Per serving: 74 Calories, 4 g Total Fat, 2 g Saturated Fat, 14 mg Cholesterol, 182 mg Sodium, 4 g Total Carbohydrate, 0 g Dietary Fiber, 6 g Protein, 186 mg Calcium

SOUPS

Fish Ball Soup (Sopa de Albòndigas de Pescado)
Sopa de Albòndigas
Chick-Pea Soup
Tortilla Soup
Black Bean Soup
Clam and Shrimp Soup
Smoky Tomato Soup
Wild Mushroom Broth
Green Corn Soup
Spicy Crab Soup
Swiss Chard with Dumplings Soup
Quick Chicken Broth
Bean Broth with Noodles

Fish Ball Soup (Sopa de Albòndigas de Pescado)

Serve this delicate soup as a first course, or add Mexican Corn Bread (see page 148) or tortillas and a salad for a light supper. A food processor or blender makes it surprisingly easy to prepare.

Makes 4 servings

Fish Balls:

10 ounces scallops
1/2 medium tomato, finely chopped
1/4 cup minced onion

2 tablespoons all-purpose flour
2 tablespoons egg substitute
1/2 teaspoon dried oregano leaves

Broth:

2 teaspoons vegetable oil
2 cups thinly sliced white onions
1/2 cup thinly sliced carrot
1/2 cup diced celery
1 medium poblano pepper, roasted, peeled, seeded and sliced (see page v; see page ix for roasting technique)
1 garlic clove, crushed
4 cups clam juice

2 cups stewed tomatoes
Two 2 × 1/2" strips orange zest*
1 bay leaf
1/4 teaspoon dried thyme leaves
1/4 teaspoon dried marjoram leaves
1/4 teaspoon ground aniseed
2 tablespoons minced fresh cilantro
1 lime, quartered

1. To prepare fish balls, in food processor or blender, combine scallops, tomato, onion, flour, egg substitute and oregano; with on-off motion, pulse processor until mixture is chunky-smooth (do not purée). Transfer mixture to small bowl; refrigerate, covered, until chilled.

2. Meanwhile, to prepare broth, in medium saucepan, heat oil; add onions. Cook over medium heat, stirring frequently, 10 minutes, until onions are golden brown. Add carrot, celery, pepper and garlic; cook, stirring frequently, 4 minutes.

3. Add juice, tomatoes, zest, bay leaf, thyme, marjoram and aniseed to vegetable mixture; bring liquid to a boil. Reduce heat to low; simmer 15 minutes.

4. With tablespoon, one at a time, spoon 16 portions of chilled scallop mixture into simmering broth (scallop mixture will be soft). Return liquid to a simmer; cook 10 minutes, until fish balls are firm and cooked through.

5. Place 4 fish balls into each of 4 large bowls. Remove and discard bay leaves and zest from broth; stir in cilantro. Ladle broth evenly into bowls; serve with lime quarters to squeeze into soup at the table.

Each serving (4 fish balls + 1¹/₂ cups broth) provides: ¹/₂ Fat, 3¹/₄ Vegetables, 1 Protein, 35 Optional Calories

Per serving: 197 Calories, 3 g Total Fat, 0 g Saturated Fat, 23 mg Cholesterol, 997 mg Sodium, 27 g Total Carbohydrate, 6 g Dietary Fiber, 17 g Protein, 143 mg Calcium

* *The zest of the orange is the peel without any of the pith (white membrane). To remove zest from orange, use a zester or vegetable grater; wrap orange in plastic wrap and refrigerate for use at another time.*

Sopa de Albòndigas

This soup has a "kick"! If you prefer a milder flavor, use mild chili powder and salsa, and substitute plain Monterey Jack cheese for the jalapeño variety.

Makes 4 servings

8 ounces lean ground turkey breast or lean ground beef (10% or less fat)

$1/2$ cup finely chopped onion

2 tablespoons minced fresh cilantro

1 teaspoon hot chili powder

1 tablespoon + 1 teaspoon vegetable oil

Two 6" corn tortillas, cut into $1/2$" pieces

2 large garlic cloves, minced

4 cups low-sodium chicken broth

1 cup fresh or frozen corn kernels (see page x for fresh corn preparation technique)

$1/2$ cup prepared thick and chunky hot salsa

$1/4$ teaspoon ground cumin

$1^1/2$ ounces Monterey Jack cheese with jalapeño peppers, coarsely shredded

1. Preheat broiler. Spray rack in broiler pan with nonstick cooking spray.
2. In medium bowl combine turkey, 1 tablespoon of the onion, 1 tablespoon of the cilantro and the chili powder, mixing thoroughly; shape into sixteen 1" meatballs. Place meatballs on prepared rack; broil 4" from heat 8 minutes, until browned. Remove from broiler; set aside.
3. In medium saucepan, heat oil; add tortilla pieces and garlic. Cook over medium-high heat, stirring frequently, until tortilla pieces are soft. Add broth, corn, salsa, cumin, remaining $1/4$ cup + 3 tablespoons onion, remaining tablespoon cilantro and reserved meatballs; bring liquid to a boil. Reduce heat to medium; cook, stirring occasionally, 10 minutes, until meatballs are cooked through and flavors are blended.
4. Ladle soup evenly into 4 bowls; serve each portion sprinkled with one fourth of the cheese.

Each serving ($1^1/2$ cups) provides: 1 Fat, $3/4$ Vegetable, 2 Proteins, 1 Bread, 10 Optional Calories

Per serving with ground turkey breast: 270 Calories, 15 g Total Fat, 4 g Saturated Fat, 53 mg Cholesterol, 592 mg Sodium, 21 g Total Carbohydrate, 2 g Dietary Fiber, 19 g Protein, 132 mg Calcium

Per serving with ground beef: 286 Calories, 17 g Total Fat, 5 g Saturated Fat, 46 mg Cholesterol, 523 mg Sodium, 21 g Total Carbohydrate, 2 g Dietary Fiber, 20 g Protein, 109 mg Calcium

CHICK-PEA SOUP

A satisfying main course, this soup is filled with the goodness of legumes and vegetables. Add Mexican Corn Bread (see page 148) or tortillas for a quick, light supper.

Makes 4 servings

1 teaspoon corn oil
2 cups chopped onions
1 cup chopped carrots
2 garlic cloves, crushed
3 cups low-sodium chicken broth
12 ounces drained cooked chick-peas (garbanzo beans)
1 tablespoon minced epazote or flat-leaf parsley
1 teaspoon pureed canned chipotle peppers in adobo sauce (see page vi for ingredient information)

$^1/_4$ teaspoon dried marjoram leaves
$^1/_4$ teaspoon dried thyme leaves
1 medium tomato, diced
1 medium jalapeño pepper, seeded, deveined and minced (see page v)
$^1/_4$ cup sliced scallions (white portion with some green)

1. In medium saucepan, heat oil; add onions and carrots. Cook over medium heat, stirring frequently, 8 minutes, until onions are lightly browned. Add garlic; cook, stirring frequently, 2 minutes longer.
2. Add broth, chick-peas, epazote, chipotle peppers, marjoram and thyme to onion mixture; bring liquid to a boil. Reduce heat to low; simmer 20 minutes, until vegetables are very tender and flavors are blended.
3. With slotted spoon, transfer $1^1/_2$ cups of solids to food processor or blender (add a few spoonfuls of liquid if using blender); purée until smooth. Return pureed mixture to saucepan; stir to combine. Cook over medium heat, stirring frequently, just until heated. Stir in tomato, jalapeño pepper, scallion and cilantro.
4. Ladle soup evenly into 4 bowls.

Each serving ($1^1/_2$ cups) provides: $^1/_4$ Fat, $2^1/_2$ Vegetables, $1^1/_2$ Proteins, 15 Optional Calories

Per serving: 232 Calories, 6 g Total Fat, 1 g Saturated Fat, 0 mg Cholesterol, 128 mg Sodium, 39 g Total Carbohydrate, 6 g Dietary Fiber, 12 g Protein, 93 mg Calcium

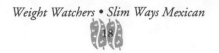
TORTILLA SOUP

This luscious soup makes a wonderful first course; for a main-meal portion, just double the serving size.

Makes 4 servings

Four 6" corn tortillas, cut into
  $^1/_4$" strips
1 medium tomato, halved
2 garlic cloves, unpeeled
1 teaspoon corn oil
4 medium dried pasilla peppers,
  seeded and torn into pieces
  (see page vi; see page ix for
  preparation technique)
1$^1/_2$ cups chopped onions
4 cups low-sodium chicken broth

4 ounces skinless boneless cooked
  chicken breast, cut into $^1/_2$"
  pieces
2 teaspoons fresh lime juice
$^1/_4$ cup nonfat sour cream
$^1/_4$ cup plain nonfat yogurt
$^1/_4$ medium avocado, peeled,
  pitted and diced
$^3/_4$ ounce Monterey Jack cheese,
  shredded
1 lime, quartered

1. Preheat oven to 325°F. Spray baking sheet with nonstick cooking spray.
2. Place tortilla strips in a single layer on baking sheet; bake 20–25 minutes, until golden brown and crisp. Set aside.
3. Preheat broiler. Line baking sheet with foil; spray foil with nonstick cooking spray.
4. Set tomato halves, cut-side down, and garlic on prepared baking sheet; broil 4–6" from heat, turning as needed, until garlic is browned and tomatoes are blistered and browned. As they are done, transfer to medium bowl; set aside to cool.
5. In medium nonstick saucepan, heat oil; add peppers. Cook over medium heat, stirring constantly, 1 minute. Transfer peppers to another medium bowl; add boiling water to cover. Let stand, covered, 20 minutes; drain and set aside.
6. Meanwhile, in same saucepan, cook onions over medium heat, stirring frequently, 10 minutes, until golden brown. Remove from heat; set aside.
7. Place reserved peppers in food processor or blender. Peel garlic; add to food processor. Add tomatoes and a few spoonsful of broth; purée until smooth.

8. Place medium sieve over saucepan with onions. Strain pepper mixture through sieve, pressing with back of wooden spoon; discard solids. Stir remaining broth into onion mixture; bring liquid to a boil. Reduce heat to low; simmer 20 minutes.

9. Add chicken to broth mixture; simmer 5 minutes, until heated. Stir in juice.

10. In small bowl, combine sour cream and yogurt.

11. Ladle broth mixture evenly into 4 bowls. To each portion, add one quarter of the reserved tortilla strips, avocado and cheese. Top each portion with one quarter of the sour cream mixture. Serve with lime quarters to squeeze into soup at the table.

Each serving (1¹/₃ cups) provides: ¹/₂ Fat, 2¹/₄ Vegetables, 1¹/₄ Proteins, 1 Bread, 50 Optional Calories

Per serving: 276 Calories, 12 g Total Fat, 3 g Saturated Fat, 30 mg Cholesterol, 236 mg Sodium, 32 g Total Carbohydrate, 3 g Dietary Fiber, 20 g Protein, 191 mg Calcium

BLACK BEAN SOUP

A classic, this satisfying soup can be dressed up by adding sherry or a lemon slice, or made into a meal with the addition of sliced hard-cooked egg and some sour cream.

Makes 8 servings

2 pounds drained cooked black beans
3¹/₂ cups vegetable broth
1 large bay leaf
6 medium tomatoes, halved
2 medium onions, unpeeled
2 medium poblano peppers (see page vi)

4 large garlic cloves, unpeeled
2 tablespoons chopped fresh epazote or cilantro
Chopped scallions (white portion with some green) or lemon slices, to garnish

1. Preheat broiler. Line large baking sheet with foil; spray foil with nonstick cooking spray.
2. In large saucepan, combine beans, broth, bay leaf and ¹/₂ cup water; bring liquid to a boil. Reduce heat to low; simmer 15 minutes.
3. Meanwhile, set tomato halves, cut-side down, onions, peppers and garlic on prepared baking sheet; broil 4–6" from heat, turning as needed, until onions and garlic are browned, peppers are blistered and tomatoes are blistered and browned. As they are done, transfer to large bowl; let cool.
4. Peel onions and garlic; place in food processor or blender. Peel and seed peppers; add to food processor. Add tomatoes; purée until smooth. Transfer mixture to saucepan with beans; return liquid to a boil. Reduce heat to low; simmer, stirring occasionally, 30 minutes, until flavors are blended. Remove and discard bay leaf.
5. With slotted spoon, transfer 2 cups of solids to food processor or blender (add a few spoonfuls of liquid if using blender); purée until smooth. Return pureed mixture to saucepan; stir in epazote.
6. Ladle soup evenly into 8 bowls; garnish with scallions or lemon slices.

Each serving (1 cup) provides: 2 Vegetables, 2 Proteins, 10 Optional Calories

Per serving: 197 Calories, 2 g Total Fat, 0 g Saturated Fat, 0 mg Cholesterol, 888 mg Sodium, 38 g Total Carbohydrate, 4 g Dietary Fiber, 12 g Protein, 51 mg Calcium

VARIATIONS:

Sherried Black Bean Soup: Add $^1/_4$ cup dry sherry along with the broth; increase Optional Calories to 15.

Per serving: 202 Calories, 2 g Total Fat, 0 g Saturated Fat, 0 mg Cholesterol, 889 mg Sodium, 39 g Total Carbohydrate, 4 g Dietary Fiber, 12 g Protein, 52 mg Calcium

"Cream-Topped" Black Bean Soup: In small bowl, combine $^1/_4$ cup nonfat sour cream and $^1/_4$ cup plain nonfat yogurt; top each portion of soup with 1 tablespoon of mixture, then garnish. Increase Optional Calories to 20.

Per serving: 207 Calories, 2 g Total Fat, 0 g Saturated Fat, 0 mg Cholesterol, 899 mg Sodium, 39 g Total Carbohydrate, 4 g Dietary Fiber, 13 g Protein, 75 mg Calcium

Black Bean–Egg Soup: Omit garnish. Slice 2 hard-cooked eggs; divide among portions of soup. Increase Protein Selections to $2^1/_4$.

Per serving: 216 Calories, 3 g Total Fat, 1 g Saturated Fat, 53 mg Cholesterol, 904 mg Sodium, 38 g Total Carbohydrate, 4 g Dietary Fiber, 13 g Protein, 58 mg Calcium

CLAM AND SHRIMP SOUP

Add Bolillos (see page 146) and a salad, and this spicy soup makes a very nice light supper.

Makes 4 servings

1 medium dried pasilla pepper, seeded and torn into pieces (see page ix for preparation technique)
1 teaspoon olive oil
1 cup chopped onions
1 ounce uncooked regular (not converted) long-grain rice
1 ounce cooked Virginia ham, diced

2 cups clam juice
2 medium tomatoes, halved and roasted (see page viii for roasting technique)
12 large steamer clams in the shell*
16 medium shrimp, brined, then peeled and deveined (see page viii for brining technique)
1/2 cup frozen green peas
1 tablespoon fresh lime juice

1. Place pepper in medium bowl; add boiling water to cover. Let stand 15 minutes; drain.
2. Meanwhile, in medium saucepan, heat oil; add onions, rice and ham. Cook over medium heat, stirring frequently, 5 minutes, until rice is lightly browned. Slowly and carefully, stir in clam juice and 2 cups water.
3. In food processor or blender, combine tomatoes and drained pepper; purée until smooth. Place medium sieve over saucepan with clam juice mixture. Strain tomato mixture through sieve, pressing with back of wooden spoon; discard solids. Stir to combine; bring liquid to a boil. Reduce heat to low; simmer 15 minutes.
4. Add clams, shrimp and peas to clam juice mixture; simmer 5 minutes, until shrimp turn pink and clams open (discarding unopened clams); stir in lime juice.
5. Ladle soup evenly into 4 bowls.

Each serving (1³/₄ cups) provides: 1/4 Fat, 1³/₄ Vegetables, 2 Proteins, 1/2 Bread, 5 Optional Calories

Per serving: 182 Calories, 4 g Total Fat, 1 g Saturated Fat, 97 mg Cholesterol, 469 mg Sodium, 19 g Total Carbohydrate, 2 g Dietary Fiber, 19 g Protein, 79 mg Calcium

* Two large steamer clams will yield about 1 ounce cooked shelled clams. To prepare clams, place them in a bowl of cold water to cover. Add a handful of uncooked cornmeal; refrigerate overnight. Drain and rinse.

SMOKY TOMATO SOUP

Make this rich-tasting soup with ripe plum tomatoes, which are available year-round. Just add some crackers and a salad and you have a satisfying light supper.

Makes 4 servings

16 large plum tomatoes, halved
2 medium onions, unpeeled
2 large garlic cloves, unpeeled
1 teaspoon pureed canned
   chipotle peppers in adobo sauce
   (see page vi for ingredient
   information)
2 teaspoons corn oil

1 cup diced zucchini ($^1/_2$" dice)
1 cup fresh or frozen corn kernels
   (see page x for fresh corn
   preparation technique)
$^1/_2$ teaspoon salt
$^1/_2$ teaspoon granulated sugar
1 tablespoon minced fresh
   cilantro or flat-leaf parsley

1. Preheat broiler. Line baking sheet with foil; spray foil with nonstick cooking spray.
2. Set tomato halves, cut-side down, onions and garlic on prepared baking sheet; broil 4–6" from heat, turning as needed, until onions and garlic are browned and tomatoes are blistered and browned. As they are done, transfer to large bowl; let cool.
3. Peel onions and garlic; place in food processor or blender. Add tomatoes and peppers; purée until smooth.
4. In large nonstick skillet, heat oil; add zucchini. Cook over medium-high heat, stirring frequently, 5 minutes, until golden brown.
5. Place medium sieve over skillet with zucchini. Strain tomato mixture through sieve, pressing with back of wooden spoon; discard solids. Add corn, salt and sugar to zucchini mixture; bring to a boil. Reduce heat to low; simmer 10 minutes, until mixture is slightly thickened and flavors are blended. Stir in cilantro.
6. Ladle soup evenly into 4 bowls.

Each serving (1$^1/_4$ cups) provides: $^1/_2$ Fat, 5 Vegetables, $^1/_2$ Bread

Per serving: 122 Calories, 4 g Total Fat, 0 g Saturated Fat, 0 mg Cholesterol, 318 mg Sodium, 23 g Total Carbohydrate, 5 g Dietary Fiber, 4 g Protein, 30 mg Calcium

WILD MUSHROOM BROTH

Try this broth as a light first course, perhaps with a slice of lemon floating on top. To bring out its intense "mushroomy" flavor, make it at least 2 hours before serving.

Makes 4 servings

1 teaspoon corn oil
$^1/_4$ cup minced onion
1 medium fresh hot chile pepper,
    seeded, deveined and minced
    (see page v)
1 large garlic clove, lightly
    crushed

1 pound wild mushrooms
    (any cultivated variety), trimmed
    and thinly sliced
2 tablespoons minced fresh
    epazote* or flat-leaf parsley
$^1/_4$ teaspoon salt
4 cups low-sodium chicken broth

1. In medium saucepan, heat oil; add onion, pepper and garlic. Cook over medium-high heat, stirring frequently, 2–3 minutes, until garlic is golden brown.
2. Add mushrooms, epazote and salt to onion mixture; reduce heat to medium-low; cook, covered, 8 minutes, until mushrooms are softened.
3. Remove and discard garlic from mushroom mixture. Add broth; bring liquid to a boil. Reduce heat to low; simmer 10 minutes, until vegetables are very soft. Remove from heat; let stand at least 2 hours or until cool, then refrigerate, covered, overnight. Reheat before serving.
4. Ladle soup evenly into 4 bowls.

Each serving (1 cup) provides: $^1/_4$ Fat, 3 Vegetables, 20 Optional Calories

Per serving: 75 Calories, 4 g Total Fat, 1 g Saturated Fat, 0 mg Cholesterol, 257 mg Sodium, 10 g Total Carbohydrate, 2 g Dietary Fiber, 6 g Protein, 32 mg Calcium

* *Epazote is a pungent herb with a long, serrated leaf. It grows wild all over the United States and is sometimes available fresh in ethnic markets.*

GREEN CORN SOUP

The "green" in this soup refers to fresh corn as opposed to dried. This is a rich, luscious soup that is a meal in itself!

Makes 4 servings

Two 6" corn tortillas, each cut into 16 wedges
1 teaspoon corn oil
$^{1}/_{2}$ cup chopped onion
1 large garlic clove, crushed
3 cups fresh or frozen corn kernels (reserve corn juices) (see page x for preparation technique)
2 large romaine lettuce leaves, coarsely chopped
3 medium tomatillos, husked and roasted (see page viii for roasting technique)

1 medium poblano pepper, roasted, peeled and seeded (see page vi; see page ix for roasting technique)
4 fresh cilantro sprigs
4 cups low-sodium chicken broth
$^{1}/_{2}$ teaspoon salt
2 tablespoons nonfat sour cream
2 tablespoons plain nonfat yogurt

1. Preheat oven to 325°F. Spray baking sheet with nonstick cooking spray.
2. Place tortilla wedges in a single layer on baking sheet; bake 15 minutes, until lightly browned and crisp. Set aside.
3. In large saucepan, heat oil; add onion and garlic. Cook over medium heat, stirring frequently, 3 minutes, until onion is tender.
4. Transfer onion mixture to food processor or blender. Add 2 cups of the corn, the lettuce, tomatillos, pepper and cilantro; purée until smooth, adding broth as necessary.
5. Return mixture to saucepan. Add remaining broth, remaining corn and juices and the salt; bring mixture to a boil. Reduce heat to low; simmer, stirring frequently, 20 minutes, until flavors are blended.
6. In a small bowl, combine sour cream and yogurt.
7. Ladle corn mixture evenly into 4 bowls; top each portion with 1 tablespoon sour cream mixture. Serve with tortilla wedges.

Each serving (2 cups + 8 tortilla wedges) provides: $^{1}/_{4}$ Fat, 1 Vegetable, 2 Breads, 30 Optional Calories

Per serving: 197 Calories, 6 g Total Fat, 1 g Saturated Fat, 0 mg Cholesterol, 439 mg Sodium, 36 g Total Carbohydrate, 5 g Dietary Fiber, 10 g Protein, 80 mg Calcium

Spicy Crab Soup

Pungent and meaty, this soup easily becomes a full meal with the addition of some rice, or serve it with crusty bread and a green salad.

Makes 4 servings

3 medium tomatoes, halved
3 garlic cloves, unpeeled
1 teaspoon olive oil
$^1/_2$ cup chopped onion
1 teaspoon pureed canned
  chipotle peppers in adobo
  sauce (see page vi for
  ingredient information)
$^1/_4$ teaspoon whole aniseed

4 cups Quick Fish Broth
  (see page 29)
Eight 2-ounce crab legs, cracked*
10 ounces shelled crabmeat, cut
  into bite-size pieces
2 tablespoons finely chopped fresh
  epazote or flat-leaf parsley
Lime wedges, to garnish

1. Preheat broiler. Line baking sheet with foil.
2. Set tomato halves, cut-side down, and garlic on prepared baking sheet; broil 4–6" from heat, turning as needed, until garlic is browned and tomatoes are blistered and browned. As they are done, transfer to medium bowl; set aside to cool.
3. In large saucepan, heat oil; add onion. Cook over medium heat, stirring frequently, 10–12 minutes, until golden brown.
4. Transfer onion to food processor or blender. Peel garlic; add to food processor. Add tomatoes, peppers and aniseed to food processor; purée until smooth.
5. Place medium sieve over same saucepan. Strain tomato mixture through sieve, pressing with back of wooden spoon; discard solids. Stir in Quick Fish Broth; bring mixture to a boil. Reduce heat to medium; cook, stirring occasionally, 15 minutes.
6. Add crab legs, crabmeat and epazote to broth mixture; cook, stirring occasionally, 5 minutes, until crab is cooked through.
7. Ladle soup evenly into 4 bowls. Serve garnished with lime wedges.

Each serving (1$^1/_4$ cups soup + 2 crab legs) provides: $^1/_4$ Fat, 1$^3/_4$ Vegetables, 2 Proteins, 30 Optional Calories

Per serving: 190 Calories, 5 g Total Fat, 1 g Saturated Fat, 85 mg Cholesterol, 540 mg Sodium, 13 g Total Carbohydrate, 3 g Dietary Fiber, 20 g Protein, 152 mg Calcium

* A 2-ounce crab leg will yield about 1 ounce cooked crabmeat.

SWISS CHARD WITH DUMPLINGS SOUP

Serve this light, but satisfying, soup in wide bowls so there is room for the little dumplings to float.

Makes 4 servings

Soup:
1 teaspoon corn oil
$^1/_2$ cup chopped onion
1 garlic clove, crushed
2 medium tomatoes, quartered
4 cups low-sodium chicken broth
2 cups lightly packed Swiss chard leaves, well rinsed and finely chopped

Dumplings:
$1^1/_2$ cups cooked regular (not converted) long-grain rice
1 egg, separated
$^3/_4$ ounce Parmesan cheese, grated
Pinch ground red pepper
$^1/_4$ teaspoon salt
1 teaspoon corn oil

1. To prepare soup, in medium nonstick skillet, heat oil; add onion and garlic. Cook over medium heat, stirring frequently, 2–3 minutes, until garlic is golden brown.
2. Transfer onion mixture to food processor or blender. Add tomatoes; purée until smooth. Return mixture to skillet; cook over high heat, stirring constantly, 5 minutes, until thickened.
3. Transfer tomato mixture to medium saucepan; stir in broth. Bring mixture to a boil; add Swiss chard. Reduce heat to low; simmer 10 minutes, until chard is tender and flavors are blended.
4. Meanwhile, to prepare dumplings, in medium bowl, combine rice, egg yolk, cheese and pepper.
5. In medium bowl, with electric mixer, beat egg white with salt until stiff but not dry; fold quickly into rice mixture.
6. In large nonstick skillet, heat oil; swirl skillet to coat. Drop rice mixture by tablespoonsful into skillet; cook 2 minutes on each side, until golden brown.
7. Ladle soup evenly into 4 bowls; add 3 dumplings to each portion of soup.

Each serving ($1^1/_2$ cups soup + 3 dumplings) provides: $^1/_2$ Fat, $2^1/_4$ Vegetables, $^1/_2$ Protein, $^3/_4$ Bread, 20 Optional Calories

Per serving: 216 Calories, 8 g Total Fat, 3 g Saturated Fat, 57 mg Cholesterol, 422 mg Sodium, 30 g Total Carbohydrate, 2 g Dietary Fiber, 10 g Protein, 126 mg Calcium

QUICK CHICKEN BROTH

This quick broth is richer and more authentic in flavor than plain canned. Freeze the broth in 1-cup portions, then thaw and heat for a light snack, or add noodles and vegetables for a quick supper when you don't feel like cooking.

Makes 4 servings

3 stalks celery, coarsely chopped
2 large carrots, coarsely chopped
1 large yellow onion, quartered
4 cups low-sodium chicken broth
1 large or 2 small plum tomatoes, quartered
1 medium dried ancho pepper, seeded (see page vi for preparation technique)
8 fresh cilantro sprigs
8 fresh flat-leaf parsley sprigs
8 whole black peppercorns, lightly crushed

Four $2 \times \frac{1}{2}$" strips orange zest*
2 large garlic cloves, peeled
2 bay leaves
2 whole cloves
One 1" piece cinnamon stick
$\frac{1}{2}$ teaspoon dried thyme leaves
$\frac{1}{2}$ teaspoon dried marjoram leaves
$\frac{1}{2}$ teaspoon dried oregano leaves
$\frac{1}{4}$ teaspoon whole aniseed, lightly crushed
$\frac{1}{4}$ teaspoon cumin seeds, lightly crushed

1. Spray large pot with nonstick cooking spray; add celery, carrots and onion. Cook over medium heat, stirring frequently, 5 minutes, until onion is lightly browned.
2. Add broth, tomatoes, ancho pepper, cilantro, parsley, peppercorns, zest, garlic, bay leaves, cloves, cinnamon stick, thyme, marjoram, oregano, aniseed and cumin seeds; bring liquid to boil. Reduce heat to low; simmer, covered, 30 minutes. Remove from heat; let stand, uncovered, 30 minutes longer. Strain; discard solids.

Each serving (1 cup) provides: 20 Optional Calories

Per serving: 20 Calories, 2 g Total Fat, 1 g Saturated Fat, 0 mg Cholesterol, 127 mg Sodium, 6 g Total Carbohydrate, 1 g Dietary Fiber, 4 g Protein, 44 mg Calcium

* The zest of the orange is the peel without any of the pith (white membrane). To remove zest from orange, use a zester or side of a vegetable grater; wrap orange in plastic wrap and refrigerate for use at another time.

VARIATIONS:

Quick Vegetable Broth: Substitute 3^1/$_2$ cups water, ^{1}/$_2$ cup tomato or mixed vegetable juice and 1 teaspoon salt for the chicken broth.

Each serving (1 cup) provides: ^{1}/$_4$ Vegetable

Per serving: 27 Calories, 0 g Total Fat, 0 g Saturated Fat, 0 mg Cholesterol, 673 mg Sodium, 6 g Total Carbohydrate, 1 g Dietary Fiber, 1 g Protein, 34 mg Calcium

Quick Fish Broth: Substitute 2 cups clam juice, 1^1/$_2$ cups water and ^{1}/$_2$ cup dry white wine for the chicken broth.

Each serving (1 cup) provides: 30 Optional Calories

Per serving: 30 Calories, 2 g Total Fat, 0 g Saturated Fat, 0 mg Cholesterol, 272 mg Sodium, 5 g Total Carbohydrate, 1 g Dietary Fiber, 1 g Protein, 46 mg Calcium

Quick Beef Broth: Substitute 3^1/$_2$ cups water, ^{1}/$_2$ cup tomato juice and 2 beef bouillon cubes for the chicken broth.

Each serving (1 cup) provides: ^{1}/$_2$ Vegetable, 5 Optional Calories

Per serving: 30 Calories, 2 g Total Fat, 0 g Saturated Fat, 0 mg Cholesterol, 555 mg Sodium, 6 g Total Carbohydrate, 1 g Dietary Fiber, 1 g Protein, 30 mg Calcium

BEAN BROTH WITH NOODLES

Use home-cooked beans in this satisfying soup; their special flavor and texture will make the soup even more delicious.

Makes 4 servings

2 teaspoons corn oil
3 ounces uncooked vermicelli pasta, broken into 2" pieces
2 medium tomatoes, quartered
$^1/_4$ cup coarsely chopped onion
1 garlic clove, peeled
3 cups low-sodium chicken broth
8 ounces drained cooked pinto or pink beans

1 teaspoon pureed canned chipotle peppers in adobo sauce (see page vi for ingredient information)
$^1/_4$ cup minced scallions (white portion with some green)
$^3/_4$ ounce Romano cheese, grated
2 tablespoons minced fresh flat-leaf parsley

1. In medium nonstick skillet, heat 1 teaspoon of the oil; add vermicelli. Cook over medium heat, stirring frequently, 3 minutes, until vermicelli is golden brown. With slotted spoon, transfer vermicelli to medium saucepan; set aside.
2. In food processor or blender, combine tomatoes, onion and garlic; purée until smooth.
3. In same skillet, heat remaining 1 teaspoon oil; add tomato mixture. Cook over high heat, stirring constantly, 3 minutes, until mixture is thickened. Add to vermicelli.
4. In food processor or blender, combine broth and beans; purée until smooth. Add broth mixture and peppers to vermicelli mixture; bring mixture to a boil. Reduce heat to low; simmer, stirring occasionally, 10 minutes, until vermicelli is tender and flavors are blended.
5. Ladle broth mixture into 4 bowls; top each portion with one quarter of the scallions, cheese and parsley.

Each serving (1$^1/_2$ cups) provides: $^1/_2$ Fat, 1$^1/_4$ Vegetables, 1$^1/_4$ Proteins, 1 Bread, 15 Optional Calories

Per serving: 242 Calories, 6 g Total Fat, 1 g Saturated Fat, 6 mg Cholesterol, 180 mg Sodium, 37 g Total Carbohydrate, 4 g Dietary Fiber, 12 g Protein, 102 mg Calcium

POULTRY

Pollo Pibil
Crunchy Taco Chip Chicken
Chicken-Corn Casserole
Pollo Borracho (Drunken Chicken)
Chicken Tamales with Molé Poblano
Mancha Manteles
Chicken-Stuffed Chile Peppers with Tomato-Cheese Sauce
Arroz con Pollo
Chicken Picadillo
Mini Tostadas with Shredded Chicken Topping
Chicken Quesadillas with Corn-Tomato Salsa
Turkey Fajitas for a Crowd
Turkey Molé Poblano
Tamale Casserole
Mexican Chili Hash in Corn Cups
Ziti Mexicana
Turkey Quesadilla
Grilled Game Hens

POLLO PIBIL

You'll have to plan in advance to serve this Yucatán classic, which should be started two days before serving. It is customarily baked in banana leaves, which lend a distinctive flavor, but foil works just fine, and the highly flavored marinade is well worth the trouble. Serve this with the traditional accompaniment of Pickled Onions (see page 168) and rice to soak up the juices.

Makes 4 servings

Achiote Paste:
1¹/₂ teaspoons achiote seeds
  (see page vii for ingredient
  information)
1 teaspoon coriander seeds
1 teaspoon salt
¹/₂ teaspoon whole black
  peppercorns

¹/₂ teaspoon ground cinnamon
¹/₂ teaspoon dried oregano leaves
¹/₄ teaspoon cumin seeds
2 whole cloves
1 tablespoon cider vinegar
2 large garlic cloves, crushed
¹/₂ teaspoon all-purpose flour

Chicken:
1 tablespoon fresh lime juice
1 tablespoon grapefruit juice
1 tablespoon fresh orange juice
2 teaspoons grated orange zest*
15 ounces skinless boneless
  chicken breast, cut into
  1" pieces

Vegetables:
1 teaspoon corn oil
1 cup thinly sliced onions
2 medium fresh hot chile peppers,
  roasted, peeled, seeded and
  sliced (see page v; see page ix for
  roasting technique)
1 medium tomato, cut into
  4 equal slices

1. To prepare achiote paste, in spice mill or mini-jar of blender, combine achiote and coriander seeds, salt, peppercorns, cinnamon, oregano, cumin seeds and cloves; process to a coarse powder.
2. Transfer spice mixture to small bowl. Add vinegar, garlic and flour; stir to combine. Let mixture stand overnight.
3. To prepare chicken, in gallon-size sealable plastic bag, combine prepared achiote paste, the lime juice, grapefruit juice, orange juice and zest; add chicken. Seal bag, squeezing out air; turn to coat chicken. Refrigerate overnight, turning bag occasionally.

4. To prepare vegetables, in medium nonstick skillet, heat oil; add onions. Cook over medium heat, stirring frequently, 10–12 minutes, until onion is golden brown. Stir in peppers; remove from heat.

5. Preheat oven to 350°F. Line baking sheet with foil. Cut four 12" squares of heavy-duty foil; spray with nonstick cooking spray.

6. Drain chicken; discard marinade. On each prepared foil square, place one quarter of the chicken, one quarter of the onion-pepper mixture and 1 tomato slice. Fold sides of foil over filling, crimping to seal; crimp ends to seal. Place foil packets on prepared baking sheet; bake 20 minutes, until chicken is cooked through. Let stand 10 minutes; open packets carefully.

Each serving (1 packet) provides: ¹/₂ Fat, 1¹/₂ Vegetables, 5 Optional Calories

Per serving: 207 Calories, 6 g Total Fat, 1 g Saturated Fat, 72 mg Cholesterol, 621 mg Sodium, 11 g Total Carbohydrate, 2 g Dietary Fiber, 28 g Protein, 49 mg Calcium

* The zest of the orange is the peel without any of the pith (white membrane). To remove zest from orange, use a zester or the side of a vegetable grater.

CRUNCHY TACO CHIP CHICKEN

Crunchy taco shells take the place of higher-in-fat store-bought chips, supplying all the goodness and none of the guilt. And the microwave oven will help you fix the chicken in almost no time!

Makes 4 servings

Four 3-ounce skinless boneless chicken breasts

1 cup chopped scallions (white portion with some green)

1 cup chopped red bell pepper

$^1/_2$ cup chopped celery

1 tablespoon + 1 teaspoon reduced-calorie tub margarine

$1^1/_2$ cups low-sodium stewed tomatoes

4 taco shells ($1^1/_2$ ounces), coarsely crushed

12 large or 20 small pimiento-stuffed green olives, chopped

$1^1/_2$ ounces sharp cheddar cheese, shredded

1. In $1^1/_2$-quart microwave-safe casserole, arrange chicken with thicker parts toward outside; microwave on High (100% power), covered, 8–10 minutes, until chicken is cooked through. Remove chicken from casserole; set aside.
2. In same casserole, combine scallions, bell pepper, celery and margarine; microwave on High, uncovered, stirring once, 3–4 minutes, until vegetables are tender. Add tomatoes; microwave on High, stirring once, 5–7 minutes, until mixture is slightly thickened.
3. Arrange chicken on top of tomato mixture; sprinkle evenly with crushed taco shells, olives and cheese. Microwave on High, 2 minutes, until cheese is melted and mixture is heated.

Each serving provides: 1 Fat, 2 Vegetables, $2^1/_2$ Proteins, $^1/_2$ Bread, 10 Optional Calories

Per serving: 261 Calories, 11 g Total Fat, 3 g Saturated Fat, 60 mg Cholesterol, 603 mg Sodium, 18 g Total Carbohydrate, 4 g Dietary Fiber, 25 g Protein, 174 mg Calcium

CHICKEN-CORN CASSEROLE

When you have a supply of Molé Poblano in the freezer, you have the basis for all sorts of delicious, quick meals. This pretty, savory casserole makes an excellent supper dish served with some warm corn tortillas and a simple salad.

Makes 4 servings

1 teaspoon corn oil
Four 3-ounce skinless boneless
   chicken breasts
$^1/_4$ cup minced onion
2 large garlic cloves, sliced
2 cups stewed tomatoes
1 cup low-sodium chicken broth

3 tablespoons uncooked yellow
   cornmeal
$^1/_2$ teaspoon dried thyme leaves
$1^1/_2$ ounces Monterey Jack cheese,
   shredded
2 servings ($^1/_2$ cup) Molé Poblano
   (see page 156)

1. Preheat oven to 350°F. Spray 1-quart shallow baking dish with nonstick cooking spray.
2. In medium nonstick skillet, heat oil; add chicken. Cook over medium-high heat, turning once, 4 minutes, until golden brown on both sides. Remove chicken from skillet; set aside.
3. In same skillet, cook onion over medium heat, stirring frequently, 8–10 minutes, until lightly browned. Add garlic; cook, stirring frequently, 2 minutes longer.
4. Transfer onion mixture to food processor or blender. Add tomatoes; purée until smooth. Return mixture to skillet.
5. In small bowl, with wire whisk, combine broth and cornmeal. Stir broth mixture and thyme into tomato mixture; bring mixture to a boil. Reduce heat to medium-low; cook, stirring frequently, 10 minutes, until thickened.
6. Spread tomato mixture over bottom of prepared baking dish. Top with reserved chicken; sprinkle with cheese. Bake, covered, 10 minutes, until chicken is cooked through. Drizzle mixture evenly with Molé Poblano; bake 5 minutes longer, until sauce is heated.

Each serving provides: $^1/_2$ Fat, $1^3/_4$ Vegetables, $2^1/_2$ Proteins, $^1/_4$ Bread, 45 Optional Calories

Per serving: 287 Calories, 10 g Total Fat, 3 g Saturated Fat, 71 mg Cholesterol, 528 mg Sodium, 23 g Total Carbohydrate, 4 g Dietary Fiber, 29 g Protein, 169 mg Calcium

POLLO BORRACHO (DRUNKEN CHICKEN)

This quick, elegant entrée gets its piquant flavor from sherry and tequila. Serve it with rice to soak up the savory sauce.

Makes 4 servings

$^1/_4$ cup golden raisins

1 fluid ounce (2 tablespoons) dry sherry

3 tablespoons all-purpose flour

$^1/_4$ teaspoon salt

$^1/_4$ teaspoon freshly ground black pepper

Four 4-ounce skinless chicken breasts or thighs

1 teaspoon corn oil

1 cup thinly sliced onions

$^1/_2$ ounce sliced blanched almonds

2 large garlic cloves, crushed

1$^1/_2$ cups low-sodium chicken broth

6 large or 10 small pimiento-stuffed green olives, sliced

$^1/_4$ teaspoon dried thyme leaves

$^1/_4$ cup + 1 tablespoon cider vinegar

2 fluid ounces ($^1/_4$ cup) tequila

2 teaspoons cornstarch

1 teaspoon granulated sugar

1. In small saucepan, combine raisins and sherry; cook over low heat just until mixture comes to a simmer. Remove from heat; let stand 10 minutes.
2. On paper plate or sheet of wax paper, combine flour, salt and pepper; coat skinned side of each chicken breast with flour mixture. Set chicken aside.
3. In medium nonstick skillet, heat oil; add chicken, flour-side down. Cook over medium-high heat 5 minutes, until golden brown. Turn chicken over; cook 3 minutes longer. Remove chicken from skillet; set aside.
4. In same skillet, cook onions over medium heat, stirring frequently, 8–10 minutes, until lightly browned. Add almonds and garlic; cook, stirring frequently, 3 minutes, until almonds are golden brown.
5. Add broth, olives, thyme and reserved raisin mixture; increase heat to high. Cook, stirring occasionally, until liquid is reduced in volume by about a third, about 10–15 minutes.
6. In small bowl, with wire whisk, combine vinegar, tequila, cornstarch and sugar; add to broth mixture. Bring liquid to a boil; reduce heat to low. Cook, stirring occasionally, until slightly thickened. Add reserved chicken; simmer, basting chicken frequently with sauce, 5–10 minutes, until chicken is cooked through.

Each serving (1 chicken breast or thigh + $^1/_2$ cup sauce) provides: $^3/_4$ Fat, $^1/_2$ Fruit, $^1/_2$ Vegetable, 2 Proteins, $^1/_4$ Bread, 70 Optional Calories

Per serving with chicken breasts: 265 Calories, 7 g Total Fat, 1 g Saturated Fat, 48 mg Cholesterol, 394 mg Sodium, 21 g Total Carbohydrate, 2 g Dietary Fiber, 21 g Protein, 50 mg Calcium

Per serving with chicken thighs: 290 Calories, 11 g Total Fat, 2 g Saturated Fat, 54 mg Cholesterol, 402 mg Sodium, 21 g Total Carbohydrate, 2 g Dietary Fiber, 18 g Protein, 48 mg Calcium

CHICKEN TAMALES WITH MOLÉ POBLANO

Makes 4 servings

Chicken Filling:
10 ounces skinless boneless
  chicken thighs
1¹/₂ cups low-sodium chicken
  broth
1 serving (¹/₄ cup) Molé Poblano
  (see page 156)
¹/₄ teaspoon dried marjoram
  leaves
¹/₄ teaspoon dried thyme leaves
¹/₄ teaspoon salt

Tamal Dough:
3 ounces uncooked hominy grits
  (not instant)
¹/₂ cup + 2 tablespoons *masa
  harina* (corn flour)
¹/₂ teaspoon double-acting baking
  powder
¹/₄ teaspoon salt
2 teaspoons corn oil

Wrappers:
18 large dried corn husks,
  prepared for wrapping (see
  page ix for preparation
  technique)*

Sauce:
3 servings (³/₄ cup) Molé Poblano
  (see page 156)

1. To prepare chicken filling, in small saucepan, combine chicken and broth; bring liquid to a boil. Reduce heat to low; simmer 30 minutes, until chicken is cooked through and very tender. Remove from heat; set aside to cool.

2. With slotted spoon, remove chicken from broth; set broth aside. Finely chop chicken; transfer to medium bowl. Stir Molé Poblano, marjoram, thyme and salt into chopped chicken; set aside.

3. To prepare tamal dough, in food processor or blender, process grits until powdery. Add *masa harina*, baking powder and salt; with on-off motion, pulse to combine. With machine on, slowly add oil and all but ¹/₄ cup reserved broth. (Dough should be thick enough to hold its shape when dropped from a spoon. If necessary, add water, 1 teaspoon at a time, until desired consistency.)

4. To wrap tamales, place one eighth of the tamal dough and chicken filling on center of each of 8 corn husks; fold long sides over filling to enclose. With kitchen string, tie both ends closed, leaving room for filling to expand. (If desired, fold one or both ends over filling rather than tying ends closed.)

5. Fill large saucepan with 1" water; bring water to a simmer. Line steamer basket with 5 of the remaining husks, leaving some gaps between them. Place tamales in prepared steamer basket; cover with remaining 5 husks and clean tea towel. Steam, tightly covered, 1¹/₂ hours, adding boiling water to saucepan as needed.

6. To prepare sauce, in small saucepan, combine Molé Poblano and remaining ¹/₄ cup broth; cook over medium heat, stirring frequently, until heated. Serve tamales with warm sauce.

Each serving (2 tamales with ¹/₄ cup sauce) provides: ³/₄ Fat, ¹/₄ Fruit, 1 Vegetable, 2 Proteins, 1³/₄ Breads, 45 Optional Calories

Per serving: 355 Calories, 12 g Total Fat, 2 g Saturated Fat, 59 mg Cholesterol, 567 mg Sodium, 47 g Total Carbohydrate, 2 g Dietary Fiber, 21 g Protein, 123 mg Calcium

*Corn husks add a sweet, distinctive flavor, but if you can't get them, cut heavy-duty foil into 8 × 10" rectangles; use in place of corn husks, folding sides over filling and pinching ends to seal.

Variations:

Chicken Tamales with Salsa Chipotle: Substitute 1 serving (¹/₄ cup) Salsa Chipotle in chicken filling and 3 servings (³/₄ cup) Salsa Chipotle in sauce for Molé Poblano.

Each serving (2 tamales with ¹/₄ cup sauce) provides: ³/₄ Fat, 1¹/₂ Vegetables, 2 Proteins, 1³/₄ Breads, 15 Optional Calories

Per serving: 306 Calories, 9 g Total Fat, 2 g Saturated Fat, 59 mg Cholesterol, 459 mg Sodium, 38 g Total Carbohydrate, 1 g Dietary Fiber, 20 g Protein, 90 mg Calcium

Chicken Tamales with Ranchero Sauce (see page 158): Substitute 1 serving (¹/₃ cup) Ranchero Sauce in chicken filling and 3 servings (1 cup) Ranchero Sauce in sauce for Molé Poblano.

Each serving (2 tamales with ¹/₃ cup sauce) provides: ¹/₂ Fat, 1¹/₄ Vegetables, 2 Proteins, 1 ³/₄ Breads, 25 Optional Calories

Per serving: 310 Calories, 9 g Total Fat, 2 g Saturated Fat, 59 mg Cholesterol, 681 mg Sodium, 41 g Total Carbohydrate, 3 g Dietary Fiber, 20 g Protein, 118 mg Calcium

MANCHA MANTELES

Like many Mexican recipes, this has a whimsical name, which means "stain the tablecloth." The spicy, fruity sauce is plentiful and richly colored, so the name is accurate! Serve it on a bed of rice, and vary the fruits to suit your taste and the season.

Makes 4 servings

2 teaspoons corn oil
Eight 3-ounce skinless chicken drumsticks
2 medium dried ancho peppers, seeded and torn into pieces (see page ix for preparation technique)
$^1/_2$ ounce almonds
1 tablespoon sesame seeds
$^1/_2$ cup chopped onion
1 garlic clove, peeled
2 medium tomatoes, halved and roasted (see page viii for roasting technique)
1 teaspoon granulated sugar
$^1/_2$ teaspoon ground cinnamon
Pinch ground cloves

6 ounces peeled yellow-ripe plantain, cut into $^1/_4$" slices (see page vii for ingredient information)
4 ounces sweet potato, pared and diced
1 small Granny Smith apple, pared, cored and diced
1 small pear, pared, cored and diced
1 cup low-sodium chicken broth
$^1/_2$ cup drained canned pineapple chunks (no sugar added), reserve 2 tablespoons juice
2 teaspoons cider vinegar
$^1/_2$ teaspoon salt

1. In large nonstick skillet, heat oil; add chicken. Cook over medium-high heat, turning frequently, 1 minute, until lightly browned. Remove chicken from skillet; set aside.
2. In same skillet, combine peppers, almonds and sesame seeds; cook over medium heat, stirring constantly, 2–3 minutes, until sesame seeds are golden brown. Immediately transfer pepper mixture to food processor or blender; set aside.
3. In same skillet, combine onion and garlic; cook over medium heat, stirring frequently, 2–3 minutes, until garlic is golden brown. Transfer onion mixture to food processor with pepper mixture; with on-off motion, pulse processor until mixture is very finely ground. Add tomatoes, sugar, cinnamon and cloves; purée until smooth.

4. Place medium sieve over skillet. Strain tomato mixture through sieve, pressing with back of wooden spoon; discard solids. Cook over high heat, stirring constantly, 2 minutes, until very thick.

5. Add plantain, potato, apple, pear, broth, pineapple and reserved juice, vinegar, salt and reserved chicken to tomato mixture; bring liquid to a boil. Reduce heat to low; simmer, covered, 15 minutes. Remove cover; simmer, stirring occasionally, 15–20 minutes longer, until plantain and potato are tender, chicken is cooked through and sauce is thickened.

Each serving (2 drumsticks + $^1/_4$ of the fruit, vegetables and sauce) provides: $^3/_4$ Fat, $^3/_4$ Fruit, $1^3/_4$ Vegetables, 3 Proteins, $^3/_4$ Bread, 30 Optional Calories

Per serving: 376 Calories, 11 g Total Fat, 2 g Saturated Fat, 82 mg Cholesterol, 412 mg Sodium, 47 g Total Carbohydrate, 4 g Dietary Fiber, 27 g Protein, 90 mg Calcium

Chicken-Stuffed Chile Peppers with Tomato-Cheese Sauce

You can use leftover roast chicken in the stuffing for this simple, yet special, Mexican dish.

Makes 4 servings

Filling:
1 teaspoon corn oil
$^1/_2$ cup minced onion
$^1/_2$ ounce slivered blanched
  almonds
2 large garlic cloves, crushed
$6^1/_2$ ounces skinless boneless
  cooked chicken breast, finely
  shredded
1 small Granny Smith apple,
  pared, cored and diced
  ($^1/_4$" dice)

$^3/_4$ cup low-sodium chicken broth
2 tablespoons golden raisins,
  chopped
6 large or 10 small pimiento-
  stuffed green olives, sliced
1 teaspoon cider vinegar
Pinch salt

Peppers:
8 large smooth-skinned poblano
  peppers, roasted and peeled
  (see page vi; see page ix for
  roasting technique)

Sauce:
4 medium tomatoes, halved
  and roasted (see page viii
  for roasting technique)
$^1/_2$ medium onion

$^3/_4$ ounce *queso fresco*, soft-textured
  pot cheese or soaked and drained
  feta cheese, crumbled

1. Preheat oven to 350°F. Spray large shallow baking dish with nonstick cooking spray.
2. To prepare filling, in medium nonstick skillet, heat oil; add onion and almonds. Cook over medium heat, stirring frequently, 5 minutes, until almonds are lightly browned. Add garlic; cook, stirring frequently, 2 minutes longer.

3. Add chicken, apple, broth, raisins, olives, vinegar and salt to onion mixture; cook, stirring occasionally, until almost all liquid has evaporated. Remove from heat; set aside.

4. To prepare peppers, carefully slit open lengthwise; remove and discard seeds.

5. Spoon an equal amount of filling into each prepared pepper; fold sides of peppers over filling to enclose. Place stuffed peppers, seam-side down, in a single layer in prepared baking dish; bake, covered, 20 minutes, until piping hot.

6. Meanwhile, to prepare sauce, in food processor or blender, combine tomatoes and onion; purée until smooth.

7. Transfer tomato mixture to medium nonstick skillet; cook over high heat, stirring constantly, 5 minutes, until mixture is thickened and reduced in volume by about a third. Remove from heat; stir in cheese until melted. Serve stuffed peppers with sauce.

Each serving (2 stuffed peppers + $^1/_3$ cup sauce) provides: $^3/_4$ Fat, $^1/_2$ Fruit, $5^1/_2$ Vegetables, 2 Proteins, 5 Optional Calories

Per serving: 274 Calories, 10 g Total Fat, 3 g Saturated Fat, 45 mg Cholesterol, 326 mg Sodium, 30 g Total Carbohydrate, 5 g Dietary Fiber, 20 g Protein, 95 mg Calcium

Arroz con Pollo

Rice with chicken is one of the most basic dishes there is; it can be simple or elaborate, depending on the occasion, your mood and what you have on hand. This is a quick version made with cooked chicken.

Makes 4 servings

1 teaspoon corn oil

1³/₄ ounces cooked chorizo sausage, diced or chopped

6 ounces uncooked regular (not converted) long-grain rice

¹/₂ cup chopped onion

¹/₂ cup chopped red bell pepper

¹/₄ cup chopped green bell pepper

¹/₄ cup chopped celery

2 cups low-sodium chicken broth

2 medium tomatoes, halved and roasted (see page viii for roasting technique)

¹/₂ teaspoon dried thyme leaves

¹/₂ teaspoon dried marjoram leaves

¹/₂ teaspoon salt

¹/₄ teaspoon freshly ground black pepper

1–2 saffron threads*

11 ounces skinless boneless cooked chicken breast, cut into chunks

¹/₂ cup frozen green peas

1. In deep medium skillet, heat oil; add sausage. Cook over medium heat, stirring frequently, 3–5 minutes, until browned.
2. Add rice, onion, red and green bell peppers and celery; cook, stirring constantly, 5 minutes longer, until rice is lightly browned.
3. In food processor or blender, combine broth and tomatoes; purée until smooth. Stir tomato mixture, thyme, marjoram, salt, black pepper and saffron into rice mixture; bring liquid to a boil. Reduce heat to low; simmer, covered, 10 minutes, until rice is almost tender.
4. Add chicken and peas to rice mixture; cook, covered, 5 minutes. Remove from heat; let stand 10 minutes, until rice is tender and mixture is heated through.

Each serving (2 cups) provides: ¹/₄ Fat, 2 Vegetables, 3 Proteins, 1³/₄ Breads, 30 Optional Calories

Per serving: 416 Calories, 13 g Total Fat, 4 g Saturated Fat, 80 mg Cholesterol, 595 mg Sodium, 44 g Total Carbohydrate, 3 g Dietary Fiber, 32 g Protein, 59 mg Calcium

* If saffron is not available, add ¹/₂ teaspoon ground turmeric in Step 2.

CHICKEN PICADILLO

If you have leftover chicken on hand, this is an almost instant dinner. Serve it with rice and a salad of mixed greens.

Makes 4 servings

2 teaspoons corn oil

1 cup chopped onions

8 ounces skinless boneless cooked chicken breast, shredded

1 small Granny Smith apple, pared, cored and chopped

1 cup stewed tomatoes

¹/₄ cup low-sodium chicken broth

2 tablespoons raisins

2 teaspoons cider vinegar

1 teaspoon pureed canned chipotle peppers in adobo sauce (see page vi for ingredient information)

¹/₈ teaspoon ground cinnamon

1. In medium nonstick skillet, heat oil; add onions. Cook over medium heat, stirring frequently, 8–10 minutes, until lightly browned.
2. Add chicken, apple, tomatoes, broth, raisins, vinegar, peppers and cinnamon to onion mixture; cook, stirring frequently, 10 minutes, until liquid is slightly reduced.

Each serving (³/₄ cup) provides: ¹/₂ Fat, ¹/₂ Fruit, 1 Vegetable, 2 Proteins

Per serving: 192 Calories, 7 g Total Fat, 2 g Saturated Fat, 50 mg Cholesterol, 241 mg Sodium, 16 g Total Carbohydrate, 3 g Dietary Fiber, 18 g Protein, 47 mg Calcium

MINI TOSTADAS WITH SHREDDED CHICKEN TOPPING

Fragrant with spices, these tostadas are flavorful and fun to eat. Serve them with a pitcher of cold Mexican beer or Toritos (see page 191).

Makes 4 servings

Two 6" corn tortillas
1 cup diced tomatoes
1/2 cup chopped onion
1 tablespoon distilled white vinegar
1 garlic clove, peeled
1/2 teaspoon mild or hot chili powder
Pinch ground cloves

Pinch ground cinnamon
1 tablespoon dried currants
2 ounces skinless boneless cooked chicken breast, shredded
4 ounces drained cooked black beans
1/2 cup shredded iceberg lettuce
1 tablespoon + 1 teaspoon nonfat sour cream

1. Preheat oven to 350°F. Spray baking sheet with nonstick cooking spray.
2. With 2" round biscuit cutter or kitchen scissors, cut four 2" circles from each tortilla; cut remaining tortilla into bite-size pieces. Place circles and pieces in a single layer on baking sheet; bake, turning frequently, 8 minutes, until crisp and golden brown.
3. In food processor or blender, combine tomatoes, onion, vinegar, garlic, chili powder, cloves and cinnamon; purée until smooth.
4. Transfer tomato mixture to large nonstick skillet; stir in currants. Bring mixture to a boil; reduce heat to low. Simmer, stirring frequently, 5 minutes, until thickened. Add chicken; cook, stirring frequently, 5 minutes longer, until almost all the liquid has evaporated.
5. In small bowl, with fork, mash beans; spread an equal amount of mashed beans on each tortilla circle. Top evenly with lettuce, chicken mixture and sour cream; serve with remaining crisp tortilla pieces.

Each serving (2 tostadas + 1/4 of the tortilla pieces) provides: 1 Vegetable, 1 Protein, 1/2 Bread, 20 Optional Calories

Per serving: 123 Calories, 2 g Total Fat, 0 g Saturated Fat, 13 mg Cholesterol, 45 mg Sodium, 19 g Total Carbohydrate, 2 g Dietary Fiber, 9 g Protein, 54 mg Calcium

CHICKEN QUESADILLAS WITH CORN-TOMATO SALSA

This out-of-the-ordinary homemade salsa includes the hearty flavor and golden color of corn; it adds a special richness to a popular Mexican dish.

Makes 4 servings

Corn-Tomato Salsa:
1 cup cooked corn kernels
$1/2$ cup diced green bell pepper
$1/2$ cup blanched, peeled, seeded and diced tomatoes
2 tablespoons chopped fresh cilantro
2 teaspoons balsamic vinegar
$1/4$ teaspoon salt

Quesadillas:
6 ounces skinless boneless cooked chicken breast, diced
1 cup shredded iceberg lettuce
$1/2$ cup prepared thick and chunky hot salsa
Six 6" flour tortillas
$1 1/2$ ounces sharp cheddar cheese, shredded

1. To prepare corn-tomato salsa, in medium bowl, combine corn, bell pepper, tomatoes, cilantro, vinegar and salt; set aside.
2. To prepare quesadillas, in separate medium bowl, combine chicken, lettuce and salsa; divide mixture evenly among 3 of the tortillas. Sprinkle chicken mixture evenly with cheese; top each with one of the 3 remaining tortillas.
3. Spray large nonstick skillet with nonstick cooking spray; place over medium-high heat. Place 1 quesadilla in skillet; cook 3 minutes on each side, turning carefully with wide spatula, until lightly browned. Repeat with remaining quesadillas.
4. Cut quesadillas into quarters; arrange 3 quarters on each of 4 plates. Serve with reserved corn-tomato salsa.

Each serving (3 quesadilla quarters + $1/2$ cup salsa) provides: $1 1/2$ Vegetables, 2 Proteins, 2 Breads

Per serving: 297 Calories, 11 g Total Fat, 4 g Saturated Fat, 49 mg Cholesterol, 712 mg Sodium, 31 g Total Carbohydrate, 3 g Dietary Fiber, 19 g Protein, 134 mg Calcium

TURKEY FAJITAS FOR A CROWD

This spiced roast turkey breast makes a spectacular centerpiece for a buffet; slice it thin and let guests help themselves. Serve with shredded lettuce, Salsa Cruda (see page 162), Salsa Verde (see page 163), Roast Peppers with Onions (see page 129) and warm flour tortillas. Add Mexican beer, or a jug of sangria, and a platter of assorted tropical fruits for dessert.

Makes 18 servings

1 tablespoon + 1 teaspoon pureed canned chipotle peppers in adobo sauce (see page vi for ingredient information)

2 teaspoons corn oil
2 teaspoons fresh lime juice
One 4-pound 4-ounce boneless turkey breast with skin

1. In small bowl, combine peppers, oil and juice. Place turkey breast, boned-side up, on work surface; open breast. Rub pepper mixture over bone side of breast. Close breast tightly; tie securely with kitchen string. Refrigerate, covered, overnight.
2. Preheat oven to 325°F.
3. Place breast on rack in roasting pan; roast 1¹/₂ hours, until juices run clear when pierced with fork and meat thermometer registers internal temperature of 165°F. Cover loosely with foil; let stand 20 minutes. Remove and discard skin before carving.

Each serving (3 ounces) provides: 3 Proteins, 5 Optional Calories

Per serving: 112 Calories, 1 g Total Fat, 0 g Saturated Fat, 71 mg Cholesterol, 61 mg Sodium, 0 g Total Carbohydrate, 0 g Dietary Fiber, 26 g Protein, 11 mg Calcium

TURKEY MOLÉ POBLANO

According to legend, this dish was invented by Sor Andrea, a seventeenth-century nun, to honor the Viceroy of Spain. It is a delicious, subtle dish, perfect for a festive occasion. Serve it with rice, or fresh corn tortillas, and a frosted jug of sangria.

Makes 4 servings

1 pound 2 ounces turkey thighs
4 servings (1 cup) Molé Poblano
(see page 156)

¹/₂ cup low-sodium chicken broth

1. Preheat oven to 350°F. Spray 8" square baking dish with nonstick cooking spray.
2. Place turkey thighs in prepared baking dish; bake 1 hour.
3. Reduce oven temperature to 325°F.
4. Remove and discard skin and bones from turkey; shred meat or slice into thin strips. Wipe baking dish clean; arrange turkey in dish.
5. In small bowl, combine Molé Poblano and chicken broth; pour over turkey. Bake, covered, 30 minutes.

Each serving (3 ounces turkey + ¹/₃ cup sauce) provides: ¹/₄ Fat, ¹/₄ Fruit, 1 Vegetable, 3 Proteins, 35 Optional Calories

Per serving: 259 Calories, 11 g Total Fat, 3 g Saturated Fat, 75 mg Cholesterol, 215 mg Sodium, 16 g Total Carbohydrate, 1 g Dietary Fiber, 27 g Protein, 78 mg Calcium

TAMALE CASSEROLE

This twist on tamales is baked in a casserole instead of corn husks; it's easy, filling and delicious! The jalapeño pepper and hot chili powder give it the traditional Mexican heat, but you can cool it way down by substituting a milder pepper and mild chili powder.

Makes 4 servings

1 tablespoon + 1 teaspoon canola oil
1 cup chopped green bell pepper
1 cup chopped onions
1 tablespoon seeded, deveined and finely chopped jalapeño pepper (see page v)
1 garlic clove, minced
8 ounces lean ground turkey (10% or less fat)

1 cup low-sodium tomato sauce
1 cup fresh or frozen corn kernels (see page x for fresh corn preparation technique)
$^3/_4$ teaspoon salt
$^1/_2$ teaspoon hot chili powder
$^1/_2$ cup uncooked stone-ground yellow cornmeal
1$^1/_2$ ounces Monterey Jack cheese, shredded

1. Preheat oven to 350°F.
2. In large nonstick skillet, heat oil; add bell pepper, onions, jalapeño pepper and garlic. Cook over medium-high heat, stirring frequently, 5 minutes, until vegetables are tender. Add turkey; cook, stirring to break up meat, 3 minutes, until no longer pink.
3. Add tomato sauce, corn, $^1/_2$ teaspoon of the salt and the chili powder; bring mixture to a boil. Reduce heat to low; simmer, covered, stirring occasionally, 15 minutes.
4. Spoon turkey mixture into 8" square baking pan; set aside.
5. In medium saucepan, combine 1 cup water and remaining $^1/_4$ teaspoon salt; bring to a boil.
6. Meanwhile, in small bowl, combine cornmeal and 1 cup water. Stirring constantly, gradually add cornmeal mixture to boiling water in a thin, steady stream; continue to cook, stirring constantly, until mixture returns to a boil. Reduce heat to low; simmer, stirring constantly, 5 minutes, until mixture thickens and forms large bubbles.

7. Top turkey mixture with cornmeal mixture, spreading evenly; bake 25 minutes. Sprinkle cornmeal mixture with cheese; bake 5 minutes longer, until cheese is melted. Remove from oven; let stand 10 minutes.

Each serving provides: 1 Fat, 2 Vegetables, 2 Proteins, 1 1/2 Breads

Per serving: 301 Calories, 13 g Total Fat, 3 g Saturated Fat, 53 mg Cholesterol, 546 mg Sodium, 31 g Total Carbohydrate, 4 g Dietary Fiber, 17 g Protein, 104 mg Calcium

MEXICAN CHILI HASH IN CORN CUPS

This is a great way to serve chili, and it makes a surprisingly hearty dinner entrée.

Makes 6 servings

Chili Hash:

$^3/_4$ cup finely chopped onions
$^1/_2$ cup finely diced carrot
$^1/_2$ cup finely diced zucchini
$^1/_2$ cup finely diced red bell
   pepper
$^1/_2$ cup finely diced green bell
   pepper
2 garlic cloves, minced
$^3/_4$ cup tomato sauce
1 tablespoon ground cumin
1 tablespoon mild or hot chili
   powder

1 tablespoon tomato paste
$1^1/_2$ teaspoons dried oregano leaves
6 ounces cooked ground turkey,
   crumbled
$^1/_3$ cup finely chopped fresh
   flat-leaf parsley
2 ounces drained cooked red
   kidney beans
2 ounces drained cooked white
   kidney (cannellini) beans
10 ounces Idaho potatoes, pared
   and diced

Corn Cups:

$1^3/_4$ cups all-purpose flour
1 cup uncooked yellow cornmeal
$^1/_2$ teaspoon salt
$^1/_4$ teaspoon mild or hot chili
   powder

$^1/_4$ cup reduced-calorie tub
   margarine
$^1/_2$ cup egg substitute

Topping:

$1^1/_2$ ounces sharp cheddar
   cheese, shredded

1. To prepare chili hash, spray large nonstick skillet with nonstick cooking spray; place over medium heat. Add onions; cook, stirring frequently, 3 minutes, until onions are softened. Add carrot and $^1/_4$ cup water; bring liquid to a boil. Reduce heat to low; simmer, covered, 5 minutes, until carrot is tender-crisp.
2. Add zucchini, red and green bell peppers, and garlic to onion mixture; simmer, covered, 5 minutes longer, until peppers are tender-crisp.
3. Add tomato sauce, cumin, chili powder, tomato paste, oregano and $^1/_2$ cup water to vegetable mixture; stir to combine. Cook, covered, 15 minutes, until vegetables are tender.

4. Stir in turkey, $^1/_4$ cup of the parsley and the red and white beans; simmer, covered, 5 minutes, until heated through.*

5. Spray clean large nonstick skillet with nonstick cooking spray; place over medium heat. Add potatoes; cook, stirring frequently, 10 minutes, until potatoes are softened. Add turkey mixture; cook, stirring frequently, 5 minutes longer.

6. Preheat oven to 375°F. Spray twelve $2^3/_4$" muffin cups with nonstick cooking spray.

7. To prepare corn cups, in medium bowl, combine flour, cornmeal, salt and chili powder. With pastry blender or 2 knives, cut in margarine until mixture resembles coarse crumbs. Stir egg substitute into flour mixture, forming a soft dough; set aside, covered, 15 minutes.

8. Spoon an equal amount of flour mixture into each prepared muffin cup, pressing dough to cover bottom and sides and forming a crust $^1/_4$" thick. Flute rim if desired. Bake 20 minutes, until cups are firm and lightly browned around the edges. Transfer cups to wire rack to cool; reduce oven temperature to 350°F.

9. Spoon an equal amount of chili hash into each prepared corn cup; top each with an equal amount of cheese. Transfer muffin cups to baking sheet; bake 10 minutes, until cheese is melted and lightly browned.

Each serving (2 filled corn cups) provides: 1 Fat, $1^1/_2$ Vegetables, 2 Proteins, 3 Breads, 20 Optional Calories

Per serving: 459 Calories, 12 g Total Fat, 3 g Saturated Fat, 27 mg Cholesterol, 588 mg Sodium, 68 g Total Carbohydrate, 6 g Dietary Fiber, 21 g Protein, 121 mg Calcium

* *Recipe may be prepared ahead up to this point; cool, then refrigerate chili, covered, up to one week.*

ZITI MEXICANA

This is a perfect one-dish entrée; serve it with a tossed salad and some fruit for dessert.

Makes 6 servings

1 tablespoon olive oil	$1/4$ teaspoon freshly ground black
1 cup diced onions	pepper
1 medium jalapeño pepper,	12 ounces cooked ground turkey
seeded, deveined and chopped	breast, crumbled
(see page v)	$1^1/2$ cups evaporated skimmed
2 garlic cloves, minced	milk
$3/4$ cup diced plum tomatoes	$1^1/2$ cups cooked corn kernels
1 tablespoon mild or hot chili	9 ounces ziti macaroni, cooked
powder	and drained
2 teaspoons ground cumin	$2^1/4$ ounces sharp cheddar cheese,
1 teaspoon salt	shredded
1 teaspoon garlic powder	Chopped fresh cilantro, to garnish
$1/2$ teaspoon dried oregano leaves	

1. Preheat oven to 350°F. Spray 9" square baking pan with nonstick cooking spray.
2. In large nonstick skillet, heat oil; add onions. Cook over medium-high heat, stirring frequently, 4–5 minutes, until onions are translucent. Add jalapeño pepper and garlic; cook, stirring frequently, 1 minute longer.
3. Add tomatoes, chili powder, cumin, salt, garlic powder, oregano and black pepper to onion mixture; bring mixture to a boil. Reduce heat to low; simmer, stirring frequently, 2 minutes. Add turkey and milk; bring just to a boil. Reduce heat to low; simmer, stirring occasionally, 10 minutes longer. Stir in corn; transfer to large bowl.
4. Add ziti to turkey mixture; toss to combine. Transfer ziti mixture to prepared baking pan; sprinkle evenly with cheese. Bake 20 minutes, until browned and bubbling; serve garnished with cilantro.

Each serving (1 cup) provides: $1/2$ Milk, $1/2$ Fat, $3/4$ Vegetable, $2^1/2$ Proteins, $2^1/2$ Breads

Per serving: 471 Calories, 16 g Total Fat, 4 g Saturated Fat, 53 mg Cholesterol, 580 mg Sodium, 55 g Total Carbohydrate, 4 g Dietary Fiber, 29 g Protein, 308 mg Calcium

TURKEY QUESADILLA

Quesadillas can range from simple to intricate; this one, falling somewhere in the middle, is easy to make and fun to eat.

Makes 1 serving

One 6" flour tortilla
1 teaspoon vegetable oil
$^1/_2$ cup minced green bell pepper
$^1/_4$ cup minced red onion
$^1/_2$ teaspoon ground cumin
$^1/_2$ cup drained canned whole
   tomatoes, chopped

2 ounces skinless boneless cooked
   turkey breast, diced
1 tablespoon chopped fresh
   cilantro
Pinch salt
Pinch freshly ground black pepper
$^3/_4$ ounce Monterey Jack cheese,
   shredded

1. Preheat oven to 350°F. Spray baking sheet with nonstick cooking spray.
2. Wrap tortilla in foil; bake 8–10 minutes, until heated and softened. Remove tortilla from oven; increase oven temperature to 375°F.
3. In medium nonstick skillet, heat oil; add bell pepper and onion. Cook over medium heat, stirring frequently, 3 minutes, until vegetables are softened. Add cumin; cook, stirring constantly, 1 minute longer. Add tomatoes and turkey; cook, stirring frequently, 3 minutes longer. Stir in cilantro, salt and black pepper; remove from heat.
4. Unwrap tortilla; place on prepared baking sheet. Top tortilla with turkey mixture; sprinkle evenly with cheese. Bake 8–10 minutes, until cheese is melted.

Each serving (1 quesadilla) provides: 1 Fat, $2^1/_2$ Vegetables, 3 Proteins, 1 Bread

Per serving: 345 Calories, 17 g Total Fat, 5 g Saturated Fat, 66 mg Cholesterol, 586 mg Sodium, 24 g Total Carbohydrate, 3 g Dietary Fiber, 26 g Protein, 257 mg Calcium

GRILLED GAME HENS

These savory hens can be grilled outdoors or broiled indoors. For a simple summer feast, serve them with Guacamole (page 5), a green salad and a stack of warm tortillas.

Makes 4 servings

¹/₂ cup coarsely chopped onion	¹/₂ teaspoon dried marjoram
4 large garlic cloves, peeled	leaves
2 small bay leaves	¹/₄ teaspoon whole black
One 2 × ¹/₂" strip orange zest*	peppercorns
One ¹/₂" piece cinnamon stick	4 whole cloves
1 teaspoon salt	¹/₂ cup fresh orange juice
1 teaspoon paprika	Two 1-pound Cornish game
¹/₂ teaspoon dried oregano leaves	hens, halved†
¹/₂ teaspoon dried thyme leaves	

1. In spice mill or mini-jar of blender, combine onion, garlic, bay leaves, zest, cinnamon stick, salt, paprika, oregano, thyme, marjoram, peppercorns and cloves; process to a coarse powder.
2. Transfer spice mixture to small bowl. Add juice; stir to combine.
3. Carefully loosen skin of hens; rub juice mixture over and under skin of hens and inside hen cavity. Place hens in gallon-size sealable plastic bags; seal bags. Refrigerate hens overnight.
4. Preheat outdoor barbecue grill according to manufacturer's directions, or preheat broiler and spray broiler pan with nonstick cooking spray.
5. Grill hens over hot coals or place in prepared broiler pan and broil 6" from heat 10 minutes on each side, until golden brown and thigh juices run clear when pierced with a fork. Remove and discard skin.

Each serving (one hen half) provides: ¹/₄ Vegetable; 3 Proteins, 15 Optional Calories

Per serving: 197 Calories, 7 g Total Fat, 2 g Saturated Fat, 76 mg Cholesterol, 626 mg Sodium, 8 g Total Carbohydrate, 0 g Dietary Fiber, 25 g Protein, 48 mg Calcium

 * *The zest of the orange is the peel without any of the pith (white membrane). To remove zest from orange, use a zester or the side of a vegetable grater; wrap orange in plastic wrap and refrigerate for use at another time.*

 †*A 1-pound Cornish game hen will yield about 6 ounces cooked poultry.*

MEATS

Smothered Steak with Beans and Papaya
Ropa Vieja
Oaxacan Black Beef Stew
Beef Enchilada Casserole
Beef and Potato Tacos
Beef Picadillo
Tinga Poblano (Smoky Pork Stew)
Pork Tamales with Swiss Chard
Roast Pork in Red Chile Sauce
Chiles en Nogada (Stuffed Peppers with Walnut Sauce)
Meatball Stew
Lentils with Pork and Plantain
Garlicky Red Beans and Pork
Pork Fajitas
Spiced Roast Lamb
Drunken Beans with Chorizo
Black Bean–Sausage Stew
Scrambled Eggs Mexican Style

SMOTHERED STEAK WITH BEANS AND PAPAYA

Papaya is a tropical fruit that has a tenderizing effect on meat. Here, it also adds a delightful sweetness and an attractive color.

Makes 4 servings

1 medium papaya, pared, seeded and thinly sliced	$^1/_4$ teaspoon freshly ground black pepper
Four 4-ounce boneless sirloin steaks	1 cup chopped tomatoes
2 teaspoons olive oil	1 cup low-sodium chicken broth
1 cup sliced red onions	8 ounces drained cooked small white beans
$^1/_2$ teaspoon ground ginger	

1. Place half of the papaya slices into a 13 × 9" baking pan; top with steaks, then remaining papaya slices. Refrigerate, covered, 1 hour.
2. In large nonstick skillet, heat oil; add onions, spreading to cover entire bottom of skillet. Top onions with steaks; sprinkle evenly with ginger and pepper. Arrange papaya slices, then tomato over steaks. Add broth; bring liquid to a boil. Reduce heat to low; simmer, covered, 15 minutes, until steaks are cooked through.
3. Add beans to steak mixture; simmer, covered, 2 minutes longer. With slotted spoon, transfer steaks, papaya, onions and beans to serving platter; reserve liquid. Set steak mixture aside; keep warm.
4. Bring reserved liquid to a boil; cook 3–4 minutes, until liquid is reduced in volume by about half. Pour liquid over steak mixture.

Each serving (1 steak + $^1/_4$ of the remaining solids and liquid) provides:
$^1/_2$ Fat, $^1/_2$ Fruit, 1 Vegetable, 3 Proteins, 1 Bread, 5 Optional Calories

Per serving: 324 Calories, 10 g Total Fat, 3 g Saturated Fat, 67 mg Cholesterol, 107 mg Sodium, 28 g Total Carbohydrate, 4 g Dietary Fiber, 32 g Protein, 84 mg Calcium

ROPA VIEJA

Ropa vieja means "old clothes," an amusing name for a delicious hodgepodge of meat and vegetables. Serve it with warm tortillas, over rice, or as a taco filling.

Makes 4 servings

15 ounces boneless beef round

1¹/₂ cups low-sodium beef broth

1 teaspoon corn oil

1 cup chopped onions

2 large garlic cloves, crushed

1 medium fresh hot chile pepper, seeded and minced (see page v)

¹/₂ cup diced jicama

¹/₂ cup pared and diced chayote (see page vii for ingredient information)

¹/₂ cup cut green beans (¹/₂" pieces)

¹/₄ cup diced carrot

1 cup diced tomatoes

¹/₂ cup diced zucchini

¹/₂ cup fresh or frozen corn kernels (see page x for fresh corn preparation technique)

2 tablespoons minced fresh cilantro

¹/₄ teaspoon dried oregano leaves

1. In medium saucepan, combine beef and broth; bring liquid to a boil. Reduce heat to low; simmer, covered, 1–1¹/₂ hours, until beef is very tender. Remove from heat; set aside to cool. With slotted spoon, remove beef from broth; reserve broth. Shred beef; set aside.
2. In large nonstick skillet, heat oil; add onions. Cook over medium heat, stirring frequently, 8–10 minutes, until onions are lightly browned. Add garlic; cook, stirring frequently, 2 minutes longer.
3. Add pepper, jicama, chayote, beans, carrot and reserved broth to onion mixture; cook over medium heat, stirring, until green beans are tender-crisp.
4. Add tomatoes, zucchini, corn, cilantro, oregano and reserved beef to vegetable mixture; increase heat to high. Cook, stirring occasionally, until zucchini is tender-crisp and liquid is reduced in volume to about 1 cup.*

Each serving (³/₄ cup) provides: ¹/₄ Fat, 2¹/₂ Vegetables, 3 Proteins, ¹/₄ Bread, 10 Optional Calories

Per serving: 238 Calories, 8 g Total Fat, 2 g Saturated Fat, 63 mg Cholesterol, 80 mg Sodium, 16 g Total Carbohydrate, 3 g Dietary Fiber, 26 g Protein, 38 mg Calcium

* *To use this dish as a taco filling, cook until most of the liquid has evaporated.*

OAXACAN BLACK BEEF STEW

This rich, complex stew is made with a black molé sauce. It takes a little time, but it can be made a day or two before serving; like most stews, it will only improve. Serve it with tortillas to sop up the abundant sauce.

Makes 6 servings

Black Molé Sauce:
Two 6" corn tortillas
8 medium dried guajillo peppers, seeded and torn into pieces (reserve $^1/_4$ teaspoon seeds) (see page ix for preparation technique)
2 medium dried pasilla peppers, seeded and torn into pieces (reserve $^1/_4$ teaspoon seeds) (see page ix for preparation technique)

$^1/_2$ teaspoon whole aniseed
$^1/_4$ teaspoon cumin seeds
8 large plum tomatoes, halved and roasted (see page viii for roasting technique)
3 medium tomatillos, husked and roasted (see page viii for roasting technique)
6 large garlic cloves, roasted and peeled (see page viii for roasting technique)

Stew:
1 teaspoon corn oil
1 pound boneless beef loin or round, cut into 2" pieces
7 ounces boneless pork loin, cut into 2" pieces
2 medium onions, cut into 1" chunks
1 medium chayote, pared and cut into $^1/_2$" strips (see page x for ingredient information)

1 cup cut green beans (1" pieces)
2 cups low-sodium beef broth
1 teaspoon dried oregano leaves
$^1/_4$ teaspoon dried thyme leaves
$^1/_4$ teaspoon dried marjoram leaves
$^1/_4$ teaspoon ground allspice
3 tablespoons *masa harina* (corn flour)

1. Preheat oven to 400°F. Spray baking sheet with nonstick cooking spray.
2. To prepare black molé sauce, place tortillas in a single layer on baking sheet; bake 30–35 minutes, until dark brown and crisp. Crumble tortillas; transfer to food processor or blender.
3. In large nonstick skillet, combine reserved guajillo and pasilla pepper seeds, aniseed and cumin seeds; toast, stirring constantly, 30 seconds, until fragrant. Transfer seeds to food processor with tortillas.

4. In same skillet, toast guajillo and pasilla peppers over medium heat, turning pieces occasionally, until blistered on all sides; transfer to food processor with tortilla and seeds.

5. With on-off motion, pulse processor until mixture is ground (do not purée). Add tomatoes, tomatillos and garlic; purée until smooth.

6. Place medium sieve over medium bowl; strain tortilla mixture through sieve, pressing with back of wooden spoon; discard solids.*

7. To prepare stew, in same skillet, heat oil; add beef and pork. Cook over medium-high heat, turning as needed, until browned on all sides. With slotted spoon, transfer meat to large saucepan or Dutch oven; set aside.

8. In same skillet, combine onions and chayote; cook over medium heat, stirring frequently, 8–10 minutes, until onions are lightly browned. Add green beans; stir to combine. Remove from heat; set aside.

9. Add broth, oregano, thyme, marjoram, allspice and black molé sauce to beef mixture; bring liquid to a boil. Reduce heat; simmer, covered, stirring occasionally, 1 hour.

10. Add reserved vegetables to beef mixture; cook 45–60 minutes longer, until beef and pork are tender.

11. In small bowl, combine *masa harina* with enough cold water to make a thin paste. Add paste to simmering stew; cook 15 minutes, stirring frequently, until liquid is thickened.

Each serving provides: $4^1/_4$ Vegetables, 3 Proteins, 55 Optional Calories

Per serving: 327 Calories, 11 g Total Fat, 3 g Saturated Fat, 63 mg Cholesterol, 93 mg Sodium, 33 g Total Carbohydrate, 2 g Dietary Fiber, 30 g Protein, 104 mg Calcium

* *Recipe may be prepared ahead up to this point; refrigerate, covered, up to 1 week or freeze for up to 3 months.*

Beef Enchilada Casserole

This wonderful dish can easily be made ahead and frozen, so don't let the large number of servings frighten you. Your family will love it as much as you will, so you'll be glad you have extra for another meal.

Makes 12 servings

2 cups canned red chili sauce
2 tablespoons all-purpose flour
4 cups low-sodium tomato purée
1¹/₂ teaspoons mild or hot chili powder
15 ounces lean ground beef (10% or less fat)

¹/₄ cup dehydrated onion flakes
Twelve 6" corn tortillas, quartered
4¹/₂ ounces sharp cheddar cheese, shredded
40 small or 24 large black olives, pitted and chopped

1. To prepare sauce, in medium saucepan, stir ¹/₄ cup of the chili sauce and the flour until flour is dissolved. Gradually stir in remaining chili sauce, tomato purée and chili powder. Bring mixture to a boil over medium-high heat, stirring occasionally; cook, stirring constantly, 2 minutes, until slightly thickened. Remove from heat; let cool.
2. Meanwhile, place large nonstick skillet over medium-high heat; add beef. Cook, stirring to break up meat, 4–5 minutes, until beef is no longer pink; stir in onion flakes. Remove from heat; set aside.
3. Preheat oven to 375°F. Spray 13 × 9" casserole with nonstick cooking spray.
4. Spread ¹/₂ cup of the cooled sauce over bottom of prepared casserole. Dip 12 tortilla quarters into remaining sauce; arrange evenly in casserole. Sprinkle evenly with one third of the beef mixture, one fourth of the cheese and one fourth of the olives. Top evenly with ¹/₂ cup of the sauce. Repeat layers 2 more times.
5. Dip remaining 12 tortilla quarters into remaining sauce; arrange over sauce in casserole. Top evenly with remaining cheese, olives and sauce. Bake, covered, 35 minutes. Uncover; bake 25–30 minutes longer. Let stand 5 minutes.

Each serving provides: ¹/₂ Fat, 2 Vegetables, ¹/₂ Protein, 1 Bread, 5 Optional Calories

Per serving: 261 Calories, 9 g Total Fat, 4 g Saturated Fat, 33 mg Cholesterol, 843 mg Sodium, 34 g Total Carbohydrate, 4 g Dietary Fiber, 14 g Protein, 154 mg Calcium

BEEF AND POTATO TACOS

Known as *tacos de carne y papas* in Mexico, this dish is surprisingly mild. If you like, add your own heat the way the Mexicans do by topping the tacos with hot salsa.

Makes 4 servings

Filling:
2 teaspoons vegetable oil

10 ounces potatoes, pared and diced (¹/₂" dice)

8 ounces lean ground beef (10% or less fat)

1 large garlic clove, minced

¹/₂ teaspoon dried oregano leaves

¹/₂ teaspoon ground cumin

¹/₂ teaspoon salt

Pinch freshly ground black pepper

Tacos:
8 taco shells (3 ounces)

1 cup diced tomatoes

1 cup shredded iceberg lettuce

1¹/₂ ounces sharp cheddar cheese, shredded

¹/₄ cup nonfat sour cream

¹/₂ cup chopped fresh cilantro

1. To prepare filling, in medium nonstick skillet, heat oil; add potatoes, tossing to coat. Cook 5 minutes, until golden brown on bottom (do not stir). Add ¹/₄ cup water; bring liquid to a boil. Reduce heat to low; simmer, covered, 2–3 minutes, until potatoes are tender. Uncover; cook 1 minute longer.
2. Add beef, garlic, oregano, cumin, salt and pepper to potatoes; cook, stirring to break up meat, 4–5 minutes, until beef is no longer pink. Add an additional ¹/₄ cup water; bring liquid to a boil. Remove from heat.
3. To prepare tacos, microwave taco shells on High (100% power), 45–60 seconds, until warm. Divide filling, tomatoes, lettuce, cheese, sour cream and cilantro evenly among warm taco shells.

Each serving (2 tacos) provides: ¹/₂ Fat, 1 Vegetable, 2 Proteins, 1¹/₂ Breads, 30 Optional Calories

Per serving: 341 Calories, 17 g Total Fat, 6 g Saturated Fat, 46 mg Cholesterol, 542 mg Sodium, 31 g Total Carbohydrate, 3 g Dietary Fiber, 19 g Protein, 166 mg Calcium

BEEF PICADILLO

Quick to fix, this dish is a welcome change from the usual ground beef concoctions. Serve it over rice or with tortillas.

Makes 4 servings

2 teaspoons corn oil
3 ounces peeled yellow-ripe
  plantain, cut into $^{1}/_{4}$" slices
  (see page vii for ingredient
  information)
1 cup finely chopped onions
10 ounces lean ground beef
  (10% or less fat)
2 garlic cloves, crushed

$^{1}/_{2}$ cup tomato purée or sauce
10 large or 6 small pimiento-
  stuffed green olives, sliced
2 tablespoons raisins, chopped
$^{1}/_{2}$ teaspoon dried oregano leaves
$^{1}/_{4}$ teaspoon ground cinnamon
$^{1}/_{4}$ teaspoon salt
Pinch ground cloves

1. In medium nonstick skillet, heat oil; add plantain. Cook over medium heat, turning pieces frequently, 3–5 minutes, until golden brown. Remove plantain from skillet; set aside.
2. In same skillet, cook onions over medium heat, stirring frequently, 10–12 minutes, until golden brown. Add beef and garlic; cook, stirring to break up meat, 4–5 minutes, until no longer pink.
3. Add tomato purée, olives, raisins, oregano, cinnamon, salt, cloves, $^{1}/_{3}$ cup water and reserved plantain to beef mixture; reduce heat to low. Cook, covered, stirring occasionally, 15 minutes, until plantain is tender.

Each serving ($^{3}/_{4}$ cup) provides: $^{3}/_{4}$ Fat, $^{1}/_{4}$ Fruit, 1 Vegetable, 2 Proteins, $^{1}/_{4}$ Bread

Per serving: 220 Calories, 10 g Total Fat, 3 g Saturated Fat, 44 mg Cholesterol, 484 mg Sodium, 18 g Total Carbohydrate, 2 g Dietary Fiber, 16 g Protein, 28 mg Calcium

TINGA POBLANO (SMOKY PORK STEW)

Makes 4 servings

1 teaspoon corn oil
9 ounces boneless pork loin, cut
  into 1" cubes
1³/₄ ounces cooked chorizo
  sausage, cut into ¹/₄" slices
1 cup chopped onions
1 large garlic clove, crushed
15 ounces red potatoes, pared and
  cut into 1" dice
2 cups stewed tomatoes, coarsely
  chopped
1 cup low-sodium chicken broth
2 bay leaves
1 teaspoon pureed canned
  chipotle peppers in adobo sauce
  (see page vi for ingredient
  information)

¹/₂ teaspoon granulated sugar
¹/₂ teaspoon salt
¹/₄ teaspoon dried thyme leaves
¹/₄ teaspoon dried oregano leaves
¹/₄ teaspoon dried marjoram
  leaves
1 teaspoon cornstarch, dissolved
  in 1 tablespoon cold water
1 medium red onion, thinly sliced
¹/₄ medium avocado, peeled and
  thinly sliced
1¹/₂ ounces *queso fresco*, soft-
  textured pot cheese or soaked
  and drained feta cheese,
  crumbled (see page vii for
  soaking information)

1. In large nonstick skillet, heat oil; add pork, sausage and chopped onions.
   Cook over medium-high heat, stirring occasionally, 8–10 minutes, until
   pork and onions are lightly browned. Add garlic; cook, stirring frequently,
   2 minutes longer.
2. Add potatoes, tomatoes, broth, bay leaves, peppers, sugar, salt, thyme,
   oregano and marjoram to pork mixture; bring liquid to a boil. Reduce heat
   to low; simmer, covered, 15–20 minutes, until potatoes are tender.
3. Stir dissolved cornstarch into pork mixture; simmer, uncovered, stirring
   frequently, 5 minutes, until mixture is slightly thickened. Remove and
   discard bay leaves. Serve each portion of stew with one fourth of the red
   onion, avocado and cheese.

Each serving provides: ³/₄ Fat, 1³/₄ Vegetables, 2¹/₂ Proteins, ³/₄ Bread,
  30 Optional Calories

Per serving: 362 Calories, 15 g Total Fat, 5 g Saturated Fat, 55 mg Cholesterol, 927 mg Sodium, 37 g Total Carbohydrate, 6 g Dietary Fiber, 23 g
  Protein, 145 mg Calcium

PORK TAMALES WITH SWISS CHARD

As an innovative take on a Mexican classic, these tamales are wrapped in Swiss chard instead of the usual corn husks.

Makes 4 servings

Pork Filling:

10 ounces boneless pork loin, cubed

1 cup low-sodium chicken broth

1 small onion, peeled and halved

1 garlic clove, slightly crushed

1 teaspoon corn oil

2 tablespoons minced onion

1 garlic clove, crushed

1 1/2 cups stewed tomatoes, pureed

2 medium pickled jalapeño peppers, seeded and chopped (reserve 1 tablespoon juice)

2 tablespoons raisins, chopped

1/4 ounce chopped almonds

Pinch salt

Tamal Dough:

1 1/2 ounces uncooked hominy grits (not instant)

1/4 cup + 1 tablespoon *masa harina* (corn flour; see page viii)

1/2 teaspoon double-acting baking powder

1/4 teaspoon salt

2 teaspoons corn oil

Wrappers:

1 pound Swiss chard leaves, thoroughly washed

Boiling water

1. To prepare pork filling, in small saucepan, combine pork, broth, onion halves and slightly crushed garlic; bring liquid to a boil. Reduce heat to low; simmer, covered, 20 minutes, until pork is cooked through and tender. Remove from heat; set aside to cool.

2. Strain pork mixture; discard onion and garlic and reserve broth. With sharp knife, shred pork finely; set broth and pork aside.

3. In medium nonstick skillet, heat oil; add minced onion and crushed garlic. Cook over medium heat, stirring constantly, 2–3 minutes, until garlic is lightly browned. Add 1/4 cup of the tomatoes, the peppers and juice, raisins, almonds, salt, reserved pork and 1/3 cup reserved broth. Increase heat to medium-high; cook, stirring frequently, until most of the liquid has evaporated. Remove from heat; set aside to cool.

4. To prepare tamal dough, in food processor or blender, process grits until powdery. Add *masa harina*, baking powder and salt; with on-off motion, pulse to combine. With machine on, slowly add oil and reserved broth. (Dough should be thick enough to hold its shape when dropped from a spoon. If necessary, add water, 1 teaspoon at a time, until desired consistency.)

5. To prepare wrappers, place Swiss chard leaves in colander; pour boiling water over Swiss chard until wilted. Let drain; set aside to cool.

6. Spoon one eighth of the tamal dough on center of 8 large Swiss chard leaves (or 8 overlapping pairs of smaller leaves; reserve very small or torn leaves); spread dough less than $1/4$" thick. Spoon one eighth of the pork filling onto center of each portion of dough. Fold stem ends of leaves over filling, then fold in opposite sides and top, making 8 bundles.*

7. Fill large saucepan with 1" water; set steamer rack in saucepan. Bring water to a boil; reduce heat to medium-low.

8. Line steamer rack with a few reserved Swiss chard leaves; set bundles, seam-side down, on leaves. Cover bundles with any remaining leaves; top with a clean tea towel. Steam, tightly covered, 1 hour, adding more water to saucepan as needed.

9. Meanwhile, to prepare sauce, in small saucepan, cook remaining tomatoes over high heat, stirring constantly, 5 minutes, until slightly thickened.

10. Arrange steamed Swiss chard leaves on serving platter. Top leaves with tamales; serve with tomato sauce.

Each serving (2 tamales, $1/4$ of the leaves + $1/4$ cup sauce) provides: $3/4$ Fat, $1/4$ Fruit, $3 1/4$ Vegetables, 2 Proteins, $3/4$ Bread, 30 Optional Calories

Per serving: 289 Calories, 10 g Total Fat, 2 g Saturated Fat, 42 mg Cholesterol, 920 mg Sodium, 32 g Total Carbohydrate, 3 g Dietary Fiber, 21 g Protein, 168 mg Calcium

* Recipe may be prepared one day in advance up to this point; refrigerate bundles, covered.

ROAST PORK IN RED CHILE SAUCE

Serve this elegant roast for a special occasion with Chiles en Escabeche (see page 167) and Arroz con Leche (see page 171). Leftovers make delicious sandwiches!

Makes 12 servings

6 medium dried ancho peppers, seeded and torn into pieces (see page ix for preparation technique)
Boiling water
$1/2$ cup chopped onion
3 large garlic cloves, sliced
2 teaspoons granulated sugar
$1/2$ teaspoon ground cumin
1 bay leaf
$1/2$ teaspoon grated orange zest*
$1/4$ teaspoon dried oregano leaves
$1/4$ teaspoon dried thyme leaves
1 teaspoon corn oil

$1^{1}/2$ cups low-sodium chicken broth
$1/2$ cup fresh orange juice
$1/4$ cup cider vinegar
1 teaspoon pureed canned chipotle peppers in adobo sauce (see page vi for ingredient information)
One 2-pound 13-ounce boneless pork loin
1 cup thinly sliced red onions
1 small navel orange, sliced
6 large or 10 small pimiento-stuffed green olives, sliced

1. In medium nonstick skillet, toast ancho peppers over medium heat, stirring constantly, 30 seconds, until fragrant. Transfer toasted peppers to medium bowl; add boiling water to cover. Let stand 15 minutes.
2. Drain peppers; transfer to food processor or blender. Add chopped onion, garlic, sugar, cumin, bay leaf, zest, oregano and thyme; purée until almost smooth.
3. In same skillet, heat oil; add ancho pepper mixture. Cook over medium-high heat, stirring frequently, 3–5 minutes, until very thick. Add $1/2$ cup of the broth, the juice and vinegar; bring mixture to a boil. Reduce heat to low; simmer, stirring occasionally, 30 minutes. Remove from heat; cool to room temperature.
4. In small bowl, combine remaining 1 cup broth, $1/3$ cup of the ancho pepper mixture and the pureed chipotle peppers; cover.
5. In gallon-size sealable plastic bag, combine remaining ancho pepper mixture and pork. Seal bag, squeezing out air; turn to coat pork. Refrigerate ancho pepper mixture and pork overnight.
6. Preheat oven to 400°F. Spray roasting pan and rack with nonstick cooking spray.

7. Drain pork; discard marinade. Place pork on prepared rack; roast 10 minutes. Reduce oven temperature to 325°F; roast 1¹/₄ hours, until meat thermometer registers internal temperature of 175°F (do not overcook). Transfer roast to serving platter; keep warm.

8. Add ¹/₂ cup water to roasting pan; place pan over medium heat. Cook, stirring constantly, scraping up browned bits from bottom of pan; remove and discard any fat that rises to surface. Add reserved ancho pepper mixture; stir to combine.

9. Transfer ancho pepper mixture to small saucepan; bring to a boil. Reduce heat to low; simmer, stirring occasionally, 15 minutes.

10. Slice pork. Top pork with small amount of ancho pepper mixture; surround with red onion, orange and olive slices. Serve with remaining ancho pepper mixture.

Each serving (3 ounces pork + 3 tablespoons sauce) provides: ³/₄ Vegetable, 3 Proteins, 20 Optional Calories

Per serving: 205 Calories, 8 g Total Fat, 2 g Saturated Fat, 63 mg Cholesterol, 134 mg Sodium, 9 g Total Carbohydrate, 1 g Dietary Fiber, 24 g Protein, 47 mg Calcium

* *The zest of the orange is the peel without any of the pith (white membrane). To remove zest from orange, use a zester or the side of a vegetable grater.*

CHILES EN NOGADA (STUFFED PEPPERS WITH WALNUT SAUCE)

Although this spectacular festival dish takes a little time to prepare, the peppers can be stuffed as much as a day before serving and simply warmed in a micro-wave or slow oven. The creamy, slightly sweet sauce is served cool over the hot peppers.

Makes 4 servings

Walnut Sauce:

$^1/_2$ cup nonfat sour cream
$^1/_4$ cup skim milk
$1^1/_2$ ounces *queso fresco*, soft-textured pot cheese or soaked and drained feta cheese, crumbled (see page vii for soaking information)

1 ounce crust-trimmed white bread, diced
1 ounce walnuts
$1^1/_2$ teaspoons granulated sugar
Pinch ground cinnamon

Pork Filling:

10 ounces boneless pork loin, diced
1 cup low-sodium chicken broth
$^1/_2$ small onion, unpeeled
2 large garlic cloves, minced
1 teaspoon corn oil
$^1/_2$ cup minced onion
2 tablespoons golden raisins, chopped
1 small pear, pared, cored and chopped*

1 medium peach, pared, pitted and chopped*
$^1/_2$ ounce slivered blanched almonds
$^1/_2$ teaspoon freshly ground black pepper
$^1/_4$ teaspoon salt
$^1/_4$ teaspoon ground cinnamon
Pinch ground cloves
1 cup drained canned Italian tomatoes, finely chopped

Peppers:

8 large smooth-skinned poblano peppers, roasted and peeled (see page vi; see page ix for roasting technique)

Topping (optional):

Seeds from $^1/_2$ large pomegranate

1. To prepare walnut sauce, in food processor or blender, combine sour cream, milk, cheese, bread, walnuts, sugar and cinnamon; purée until smooth. Transfer to serving bowl; refrigerate, covered, until chilled.
2. To prepare pork filling, in medium saucepan, combine pork, broth, unpeeled onion and half of the minced garlic; bring liquid to a boil. Reduce heat to low; simmer, covered, 45 minutes, until pork is cooked through and tender. Remove from heat; set aside to cool.
3. Strain pork mixture; discard onion and reserve broth. With sharp knife, chop meat finely; set broth and pork aside.
4. In medium nonstick skillet, heat oil; add minced onion and remaining garlic. Cook over medium heat, stirring frequently, 4 minutes, until onion is softened.
5. Add chopped pork to onion mixture; cook, stirring frequently, until pork is lightly browned. Add raisins, pear, peach, almonds, pepper, salt, cinnamon and cloves; cook, stirring frequently, 2 minutes longer.
6. Add tomatoes and ¹/₂ cup reserved broth; increase heat to high. Cook, stirring frequently, 7–10 minutes, until most of the liquid has evaporated.
7. Preheat oven to 325°F. Spray large shallow baking dish with nonstick cooking spray.
8. To prepare peppers, carefully slit open lengthwise; remove and discard seeds.
9. Spoon an equal amount of filling into each prepared pepper; fold sides of peppers over filling to enclose, securing with toothpicks if necessary. Place stuffed peppers, seam-side down, in a single layer, in prepared baking dish†; bake 20 minutes.
10. Spoon pomegranate seeds over walnut sauce; serve stuffed peppers with sauce.

Each serving (2 stuffed peppers + ¹/₄ cup sauce) provides: 1 Fat, 1 Fruit, 3³/₄ Vegetables, 2³/₄ Proteins, ¹/₄ Bread, 45 Optional Calories

Per serving: 436 Calories, 16 g Total Fat, 4 g Saturated Fat, 50 mg Cholesterol, 456 mg Sodium, 51 g Total Carbohydrate, 6 g Dietary Fiber, 28 g Protein, 223 mg Calcium

* If desired, 1¹/₂ ounces mixed dried fruit, chopped, may be substituted for the pear and peach.

Per serving with mixed dried fruit: 425 Calories, 16 g Total Fat, 4 g Saturated Fat, 50 mg Cholesterol, 458 mg Sodium, 48 g Total Carbohydrate, 5 g Dietary Fiber, 28 g Protein, 221 mg Calcium

†Recipe may be prepared one day in advance up to this point; refrigerate stuffed peppers, covered. Preheat oven about 15 minutes before baking; increase baking time to 30 minutes.

MEATBALL STEW

Serve this brothy stew in bowls with crusty bread to sop up the delicious juices.

Makes 4 servings

10 ounces boneless pork loin, cubed
1/4 cup coarsely chopped onion
2 garlic cloves, crushed
1 teaspoon salt
1/2 teaspoon freshly ground black pepper
Pinch ground cloves
1 medium dried ancho pepper, seeded and torn into pieces (see page ix for preparation technique)
1 medium dried guajillo pepper, seeded and torn into pieces (see page ix for preparation technique)

Boiling water
1 teaspoon corn oil
1 cup chopped onions
2 large garlic cloves, peeled
8 ounces drained cooked chickpeas (garbanzo beans)
2 cups low-sodium chicken broth
1 cup chopped carrots
1 cup cut green beans (1" pieces)
1 medium zucchini, diced

1. To prepare meatballs, in food processor, combine pork, coarsely chopped onion, crushed garlic, 1/2 teaspoon of the salt, the black pepper and cloves; with on-off motion, pulse processor until mixture is ground (do not purée). With wet hands, form mixture into sixteen 1" balls; set aside.
2. In large nonstick skillet, toast ancho and guajillo peppers over medium heat, stirring constantly, 30 seconds, until fragrant. Transfer toasted peppers to small bowl; add boiling water to cover. Let stand 15 minutes.
3. Meanwhile, in same skillet, heat oil; add meatballs. Cook over medium-high heat, turning frequently, until browned on all sides. Transfer meatballs to medium saucepan.
4. Drain peppers; transfer peppers to food processor or blender.
5. In same skillet, cook chopped onions over medium heat, stirring frequently 8–10 minutes, until lightly browned. Add peeled garlic; cook, stirring frequently, 2 minutes longer. Transfer onion mixture to blender with peppers; purée until smooth, adding water, 1 teaspoon at a time, as needed. Pour pepper mixture over meatballs.

6. Stir chick-peas, broth, carrots, green beans, zucchini and remaining $^1/_2$ tea-spoon salt into meatball mixture; bring liquid to a boil. Reduce heat to low; simmer, covered, 45 minutes, adding additional water, 1 tablespoon at a time, if mixture becomes too thick.

Each serving (1$^1/_2$ cups) provides: $^1/_4$ Fat, 2$^3/_4$ Vegetables; 3 Proteins, 10 Optional Calories

Per serving: 293 Calories, 10 g Total Fat, 2 g Saturated Fat, 42 mg Choles-terol, 669 mg Sodium, 32 g Total Carbohydrate, 4 g Dietary Fiber, 25 g Protein, 111 mg Calcium

LENTILS WITH PORK AND PLANTAIN

This soupy stew is excellent both with and without the pork; the spices and cider give it a subtly sweet taste that is unusual and delicious. Serve it with warm tortillas or over rice.

Makes 4 servings

3³/₄ ounces brown lentils, rinsed

1 medium dried ancho pepper, seeded and torn into pieces (see page ix for preparation technique)

Boiling water

2 large or 4 small plum tomatoes, halved

2 teaspoons corn oil

¹/₂ cup chopped onion

1 garlic clove, crushed

¹/₄ teaspoon dried oregano leaves

¹/₄ teaspoon ground cinnamon

Pinch ground cloves

5 ounces boneless pork loin, cut into ¹/₄" dices

¹/₂ cup peeled and sliced green plantain (¹/₄" slices) (see page vii for ingredient information)

¹/₄ cup apple cider

¹/₂ teaspoon salt

1. In medium saucepan, bring 3¹/₄ cups water to a boil; reduce heat to medium-low. Add lentils; cook 20 minutes, until tender.
2. Meanwhile, in medium nonstick skillet, toast pepper over medium heat, stirring constantly, 30 seconds, until fragrant. Transfer pepper to small bowl; add boiling water to cover. Let stand 15 minutes; drain. Transfer pepper to food processor or blender; set aside.
3. Place tomatoes, skin-side down, in same skillet; cook, turning once, 5 minutes, until charred on both sides. Transfer tomatoes to food processor with pepper.
4. In same skillet, heat 1 teaspoon of the oil; add onion. Cook over medium heat, stirring frequently, 8–10 minutes, until onion is lightly browned. Add garlic; cook, stirring frequently, 2 minutes longer. Transfer onion mixture to food processor with peppers and tomatoes. Add oregano, cinnamon, and cloves; purée until smooth. Set purée aside.
5. In same skillet, heat remaining 1 teaspoon oil; add pork. Cook over medium heat, stirring frequently, about 10 minutes, until browned and cooked through. Transfer pork to saucepan with lentils.

6. Transfer pepper purée to same skillet; cook over high heat, stirring constantly, 2–3 minutes, until thickened. Stir thickened purée, the plantain, cider and salt into lentil mixture; reduce heat to low. Simmer, covered, stirring occasionally, 45 minutes, until lentils are very soft.

Each serving ($^3/_4$ cup) provides: $^1/_2$ Fat, 1 Vegetable, $2^1/_4$ Proteins, $^1/_4$ Bread, 10 Optional Calories

Per serving: 220 Calories, 5 g Total Fat, 1 g Saturated Fat, 21 mg Cholesterol, 300 mg Sodium, 29 g Total Carbohydrate, 4 g Dietary Fiber, 16 g Protein, 38 mg Calcium

GARLICKY RED BEANS AND PORK

Garlic lovers, this one's for you!

Makes 4 servings

1 tablespoon + 1 teaspoon olive or vegetable oil

10 ounces boneless pork loin, cut into 1 1/2" cubes

1/4 teaspoon freshly ground black pepper

1 cup chopped red onions

6 garlic cloves, minced

2 cups coarsely chopped tomatoes

6 ounces dried red kidney beans, soaked overnight, rinsed and drained

1/4 cup drained canned mild or hot chopped green chile peppers

1/2 teaspoon ground cumin

1. In large saucepan, heat oil; add pork and black pepper. Cook over medium heat, stirring frequently, 8–10 minutes, until pork is cooked through and lightly browned. Add onions and garlic; cook, stirring frequently, 8 minutes longer, until onions are tender.

2. Stir tomatoes, beans, chile peppers, cumin and 1/2 cup water into pork mixture; bring liquid to a boil. Reduce heat to low; cook, covered, 50–60 minutes, until beans are tender.

Each serving provides: 1 Fat, 1 3/4 Vegetables, 2 Proteins, 2 Breads

Per serving: 328 Calories, 9 g Total Fat, 2 g Saturated Fat, 42 mg Cholesterol, 185 mg Sodium, 35 g Total Carbohydrate, 6 g Dietary Fiber, 27 g Protein, 102 mg Calcium

PORK FAJITAS

Makes 4 servings

$^1/_4$ cup fresh lime juice
4 teaspoons vegetable oil
3 garlic cloves, minced
1 teaspoon low-sodium soy sauce
$^1/_2$ teaspoon mild or hot chili powder
$^1/_2$ teaspoon crushed red pepper flakes
$^1/_4$ teaspoon ground cumin
15 ounces boneless pork tender- loin, cut into $^1/_2$" strips

2 medium onions, thinly sliced
1 medium green bell pepper, seeded and cut into $^1/_4$" strips
1 medium red bell pepper, seeded and cut into $^1/_4$" strips
Eight 6" flour tortillas
$^1/_2$ cup prepared salsa
$^1/_4$ cup nonfat sour cream
$^1/_4$ cup chopped fresh cilantro

1. To prepare marinade, in gallon-size sealable plastic bag, combine juice, 2 teaspoons of the oil, the garlic, soy sauce, chili powder, red pepper flakes and cumin; add pork. Seal bag, squeezing out air; turn to coat pork. Refrigerate 2–3 hours, turning bag occasionally. Drain marinade; set pork and marinade aside.
2. In large nonstick skillet, heat remaining 2 teaspoons oil; add onions and green and red bell peppers. Cook, stirring frequently, 10–12 minutes, until vegetables are golden brown. Add $^1/_2$ cup water to pepper mixture; cook, stirring frequently, 5 minutes longer, until peppers are soft and liquid has evaporated. Transfer peppers to plate; keep warm.
3. In same skillet, cook half of the pork, stirring frequently, 2–3 minutes, until just cooked through. Transfer cooked pork to separate plate; repeat.
4. In same skillet, cook reserved marinade, stirring frequently, 5–8 minutes, until thickened. Stir in cooked pork; remove from heat.
5. Layer tortillas between sheets of damp paper towels; place on microwave-safe plate. Microwave on Medium (50% power) 30 seconds, until warm. Place an equal amount of pork mixture and vegetable mixture on center of each warm tortilla; top each with 1 tablespoon salsa, $1^1/_2$ teaspoons sour cream and $1^1/_2$ teaspoons cilantro.

Each serving (2 fajitas) provides: 1 Fat, $1^3/_4$ Vegetables, 3 Proteins, 2 Breads, 10 Optional Calories

Per serving: 357 Calories, 11 g Total Fat, 2 g Saturated Fat, 69 mg Cholesterol, 631 mg Sodium, 34 g Total Carbohydrate, 3 g Dietary Fiber, 28 g Protein, 96 mg Calcium

SPICED ROAST LAMB

Serve this fragrant marinated roast with fresh flour tortillas, a big mixed salad and dry red wine or sangria. Start the preparation two days before you plan to serve.

Makes 12 servings

Lamb:
6 medium dried ancho peppers, seeded and torn into pieces (see page ix for preparation technique)
Boiling water
8 large garlic cloves, unpeeled
$^1/_4$ cup cider vinegar
$^1/_2$ teaspoon salt
$^1/_2$ teaspoon freshly ground black pepper
$^1/_4$ teaspoon ground cumin
1 teaspoon granulated sugar
One 3-pound 6-ounce leg of lamb (butt end)

Sauce:
$^1/_2$ cup tomato purée
$^1/_2$ teaspoon dried oregano leaves

Topping:
$^1/_4$ cup minced onion
2 tablespoons minced fresh cilantro
Lime wedges, to garnish

1. To prepare lamb, in small nonstick skillet, cook ancho peppers over medium heat, turning frequently, 3 minutes, until blistered. Transfer ancho peppers to small bowl; add boiling water to cover. Let stand 30 minutes.
2. Meanwhile, in same skillet, cook garlic over low heat, turning frequently, 15 minutes, until charred on all sides. Cool; peel, discarding skin.
3. Drain ancho peppers; transfer peppers and garlic to food processor or blender. Add vinegar, salt, black pepper and cumin; purée until smooth, adding water, a few tablespoons at a time, to form a thick sauce.
4. Transfer $^1/_3$ cup pepper sauce to small bowl; stir in sugar. Refrigerate, covered, 2 days.
5. Meanwhile, transfer remaining pepper sauce to gallon-size sealable plastic bag; add lamb. Seal bag, squeezing out air; turn to coat lamb. Refrigerate 2 days, turning bag occasionally.
6. Preheat oven to 325°F.

7. Drain marinade from lamb into small saucepan; bring to a boil. Remove from heat; stir in $2^1/_2$ cups water. Place lamb in roasting pan; pour marinade over lamb. Roast $1^3/_4$ hours, until meat thermometer registers internal temperature of 145°F for medium-rare, 155°F for medium or 165°F for well-done. Transfer roast to serving platter; reserve pan juices and keep roast warm.

8. To prepare sauce, in medium saucepan, combine tomato purée, oregano, reserved pepper sauce and reserved pan juices; bring mixture to a boil. Cook, stirring occasionally, until mixture is reduced in volume to about 1 cup.

9. Carve lamb.

10. In small bowl, combine onion and cilantro; sprinkle over lamb. Serve lamb with tomato sauce; garnish with lime wedges.

Each serving (3 ounces lamb + $1^1/_2$ tablespoons sauce) provides: $^3/_4$ Vegetable, 3 Proteins

Per serving: 197 Calories, 8 g Total Fat, 3 g Saturated Fat, 76 mg Cholesterol, 193 mg Sodium, 7 g Total Carbohydrate, 0 g Dietary Fiber, 25 g Protein, 27 mg Calcium

DRUNKEN BEANS WITH CHORIZO

Serve this wonderful bean dish with tortillas or rice; or you can continue to cook beans until most of the liquid has evaporated, mash them lightly and use as a filling for tacos, enchiladas or burritos.

Makes 4 servings

6 ounces dried pinto or pink beans, soaked overnight, rinsed and drained

2 medium tomatoes, halved

2 large cloves garlic, unpeeled

1 medium dried chipotle pepper, seeded and torn into pieces (see page ix for preparation technique)

1 medium dried pasilla pepper, seeded and torn into pieces (see page ix for preparation technique)

$^1/_4$ cup Mexican beer or imported dark European beer

1 bay leaf

$^3/_4$ teaspoon salt

1 teaspoon corn oil

1 cup chopped onions

1 medium red bell pepper, seeded and diced

1 medium green bell pepper, seeded and diced

$1^3/_4$ ounces cooked chorizo sausage, crumbled

2 medium poblano peppers, roasted, peeled, seeded and diced (see page vi; see page ix for roasting technique)

$^1/_4$ cup nonfat sour cream

2 tablespoons minced red onion

2 tablespoons minced fresh cilantro

1. In large saucepan, bring 2 cups water to a rolling boil; add beans. Reduce heat to medium-low; cook, covered, 2 hours, until beans are tender.

2. Meanwhile, preheat broiler. Line baking sheet with foil.

3. Set tomato halves, cut-side down, and garlic on prepared baking sheet; broil 4–6" from heat, turning as needed, until garlic is browned and tomatoes are blistered and browned. As they are done, transfer to medium bowl; set aside to cool.

4. In medium nonstick skillet, toast chipotle and pasilla peppers over medium heat, stirring constantly, 30 seconds, until fragrant. Transfer peppers to small bowl. Add hot water to cover; let stand 15 minutes.

5. Drain peppers; transfer to food processor or blender. Peel garlic; add to food processor. Add tomatoes; purée until smooth. Transfer purée to saucepan with beans. Add beer, bay leaf and salt; continue cooking.

6. In same skillet, heat oil; add chopped onions, red and green bell peppers and sausage. Cook over medium heat, stirring frequently, 8 minutes, until onions are lightly browned. Transfer onion mixture and the poblano peppers to bean mixture; cook, stirring occasionally, 1 hour longer, until flavors are blended and mixture is slightly syrupy, adding more water, a tablespoon at a time, if mixture becomes too thick. Remove and discard bay leaf.

7. Divide mixture evenly among 4 bowls; top each portion with 1 tablespoon sour cream, then one fourth of the red onion and cilantro.

Each serving (1 cup) provides: $^1/_4$ Fat, $3^1/_2$ Vegetables, $2^1/_4$ Proteins, 35 Optional Calories

Per serving: 291 Calories, 7 g Total Fat, 2 g Saturated Fat, 10 mg Cholesterol, 601 mg Sodium, 45 g Total Carbohydrate, 8 g Dietary Fiber, 15 g Protein, 113 mg Calcium

VARIATION:

Drunken Beans: Omit sausage; reduce Protein Selections to 2 and Optional Calories to 15.

Per serving: 246 Calories, 3 g Total Fat, 0 g Saturated Fat, 0 mg Cholesterol, 440 mg Sodium, 45 g Total Carbohydrate, 8 g Dietary Fiber, 13 g Protein, 109 mg Calcium

Black Bean–Sausage Stew

Serve this hearty stew with Torta de Arroz con Elote (see page 154) and a crisp salad for a comforting supper on a cold night.

Makes 4 servings

3 medium tomatoes, halved

2 large garlic cloves, unpeeled

8 ounces drained cooked black beans

1 cup vegetable broth

1 medium dried guajillo or pasilla pepper, seeded (see page ix for preparation technique)

1 teaspoon corn oil

1 cup chopped onions

1³/₄ ounces cooked chorizo sausage, sliced or chopped

10 ounces red potatoes, pared and diced (¹/₂" dice)

¹/₂ cup diced carrot

¹/₄ cup diced celery

1 teaspoon pureed canned chipotle peppers in adobo sauce (see page vi for ingredient information)

¹/₄ teaspoon salt

2 hard-cooked eggs, peeled and sliced

1 medium jalapeño pepper, seeded, deveined and minced (see page v)

2 tablespoons sliced scallions (white portion with some green)

2 tablespoons minced fresh cilantro

1. Preheat broiler. Line baking sheet with foil; spray with nonstick cooking spray.
2. Set tomato halves, cut-side down, and garlic on prepared baking sheet; broil 4–6" from heat, turning as needed, until garlic is browned and tomatoes are blistered and browned. As they are done, transfer to medium bowl; set aside to cool.
3. In medium saucepan, combine beans and broth; bring liquid to a simmer.
4. Meanwhile, in small nonstick skillet, toast guajillo pepper over medium heat, stirring constantly, 30 seconds, until fragrant. Transfer pepper to small bowl. Add hot water to cover; let stand 10 minutes.
5. Drain pepper; transfer to food processor or blender. Peel garlic; add to food processor. Add tomatoes; purée until smooth. Transfer purée to saucepan with simmering beans; continue simmering.
6. In same skillet, heat oil; add onions and sausage. Cook over medium heat, stirring frequently, 8 minutes, until onions are lightly browned. Transfer onion mixture, the potatoes, carrot, celery, chipotle peppers and salt to simmering bean mixture; simmer, covered, stirring occasionally, 30 minutes longer, until vegetables are tender and flavors are blended.

7. Divide mixture evenly among 4 bowls; top each portion with one fourth of the egg slices, jalapeño pepper, scallions and cilantro.

Each serving (1$^1/_4$ cups) provides: $^1/_4$ Fat, 3 Vegetables, 1$^3/_4$ Proteins, $^1/_2$ Bread, 25 Optional Calories

Per serving: 299 Calories, 10 g Total Fat, 3 g Saturated Fat, 117 mg Cholesterol, 626 mg Sodium, 42 g Total Carbohydrate, 5 g Dietary Fiber, 14 g Protein, 67 mg Calcium

VARIATION:

Black Bean Stew: Omit chorizo; reduce Protein Selections to 1$^1/_2$ and Optional Calories to 5.

Per serving: 253 Calories, 6 g Total Fat, 1 g Saturated Fat, 106 mg Cholesterol, 465 mg Sodium, 42 g Total Carbohydrate, 5 g Dietary Fiber, 12 g Protein, 63 mg Calcium

SCRAMBLED EGGS MEXICAN STYLE

Serve these delicious scrambled eggs with cinnamon toast and fresh fruit for a quick, impromptu brunch. Or make them the centerpiece of a more lavish spread with Torta de Arroz con Elote (see page 154) and Jicama-Fruit Salad (see page 123).

Makes 4 servings

$^1/_2$ cup minced onion	1 cup egg substitute
$1^3/_4$ ounces cooked chorizo sausage, diced	2 eggs
	Pinch salt
1 cup finely chopped tomatoes	2 tablespoons minced fresh flat-leaf
1 medium poblano pepper, roasted, peeled, seeded and diced (see page vi; see page ix for roasting technique)	parsley or cilantro

1. In medium nonstick skillet, combine onion and sausage; cook over medium heat, stirring frequently, 10–12 minutes, until onion is golden brown.
2. Add tomatoes and pepper to onion mixture; increase heat to medium-high. Cook, stirring frequently, 2 minutes, until most of the liquid has evaporated; reduce heat to low.
3. In small bowl, with wire whisk, combine egg substitute, eggs and 1 tablespoon water. Add egg mixture to tomato mixture; cook, stirring gently and occasionally with spatula, 3–5 minutes, to form large curds (do not overcook). Sprinkle egg mixture with salt, then transfer to serving platter. Serve sprinkled with parsley.

Each serving provides: 1 Vegetable, $1^3/_4$ Proteins, 20 Optional Calories

Per serving: 137 Calories, 7 g Total Fat, 2 g Saturated Fat, 117 mg Cholesterol, 331 mg Sodium, 7 g Total Carbohydrate, 1 g Dietary Fiber, 13 g Protein, 48 mg Calcium

5

SEAFOOD

Red Snapper with Tomatoes, Capers and Olives
Fish and Oyster Escabeche
Fish with Toasted Garlic and Lime
Fish Grilled in Corn Husks
Savory Cilantro Salmon
Salmon-Mackerel Seviche
Shrimp with Garlic and Spinach
Spicy Shrimp with Black Bean Salsa
Mini Tostadas with Cilantro-Shrimp Topping
Scallop Seviche
Broiled Shark Steaks with Roast Pepper Cream
Calamares en su Tinta (Squid in Its Own Ink)

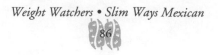
RED SNAPPER WITH TOMATOES, CAPERS AND OLIVES

This classic from Veracruz has a light tomato sauce that accents rather than masks the flavor of fresh fish; serve it with rice or fresh flour tortillas.

Makes 4 servings

Broth:

¹/₂ cup clam juice
¹/₂ cup chopped tomato
¹/₄ cup coarsely chopped onion
¹/₄ cup chopped carrot
¹/₄ cup chopped celery
¹/₂ medium fresh hot chile pepper, seeded and deveined (see page v)

One 2 × ¹/₂" strip orange zest*
¹/₄ teaspoon dried thyme leaves
¹/₄ teaspoon dried marjoram leaves
Pinch whole aniseed

Fish:

Four 5-ounce red snapper fillets, each ¹/₂" thick
2 tablespoons fresh lime juice
1 tablespoon olive oil
2 cups thinly sliced onions
2 garlic cloves, crushed
3 cups drained canned Italian tomatoes, chopped
6 large or 10 small pitted green olives, sliced
2 medium pickled jalapeño peppers, seeded and sliced (with 1 tablespoon juice)

2 tablespoons drained capers
3 bay leaves
One 1" piece cinnamon stick
¹/₂ teaspoon dried thyme leaves
¹/₂ teaspoon dried marjoram leaves
¹/₄ teaspoon coarsely ground black pepper
Pinch ground cloves
2 tablespoons minced fresh flat-leaf parsley

1. To prepare broth, in medium saucepan, combine juice, tomato, coarsely chopped onion, carrot, celery, chile pepper, zest, thyme, marjoram and aniseed; bring liquid to a boil. Reduce heat to low; simmer, covered, 20 minutes. Strain; set aside.

2. To prepare fish, on medium nonreactive dish,† sprinkle fish with lime juice; refrigerate, covered, 1 hour.

3. Meanwhile, in large skillet with heatproof or removable handle, heat oil; add thinly sliced onions. Cook over medium heat, stirring frequently, 8–10 minutes, until onions are lightly browned. Stir in garlic; cook, stirring frequently, 1 minute longer.

4. Add tomatoes, olives, jalapeño peppers and reserved juice, 1 tablespoon of the capers, the bay leaves, cinnamon, thyme, marjoram, black pepper, cloves and ¹/₂ cup of the reserved broth; bring liquid to a boil. Reduce heat to low; simmer, stirring occasionally, 15 minutes. Remove and discard garlic, cinnamon stick and bay leaves.

5. Preheat oven to 350°F.

6. Drain and rinse fish; arrange fish, skin-side down, in skillet, spooning sauce over fillets. Bake, covered, 8–10 minutes, until fish flakes easily when tested with fork.

7. Transfer fish and sauce to serving platter; sprinkle with remaining 1 tablespoon capers and the parsley.

Each serving (1 fish fillet + ³/₄ cup sauce) provides: 1 Fat, 3 Vegetables, 2 Proteins

Per serving: 278 Calories, 7 g Total Fat, 1 g Saturated Fat, 52 mg Cholesterol, 877 mg Sodium, 20 g Total Carbohydrate, 4 g Dietary Fiber, 33 g Protein, 153 mg Calcium

* *The zest of the orange is the peel without any of the pith (white membrane). To remove zest from orange, use a zester or side of a vegetable grater; wrap orange in plastic wrap and refrigerate for use at another time.*

† *It's best to marinate in bowls made of nonreactive material, such as glass, stainless steel or ceramic; ingredients such as lime juice may react with other materials, causing color and flavor changes in foods.*

FISH AND OYSTER ESCABECHE

Serve this fresh-tasting seafood dish either hot or cold. For a simple dinner, just add some crusty bread and a glass of dry white wine.

Makes 4 servings

2 bay leaves
$^1/_2$ teaspoon whole black peppercorns
$^1/_2$ teaspoon dried oregano leaves
4 whole cloves
$^1/_4$ teaspoon cumin seeds
$^1/_4$ teaspoon whole allspice
$^1/_4$ cup cider vinegar
$^1/_4$ cup clam juice
10 ounces red snapper, halibut or bass fillets, cut into 8 equal pieces
2 teaspoons all-purpose flour

2 teaspoons olive oil
$1^1/_2$ cups thinly sliced onions
1 cup thinly sliced carrots
4 medium fresh hot chile peppers, roasted, peeled, seeded and sliced (see page v; see page ix for roasting technique)
4 large garlic cloves, crushed
24 medium oysters in the shell, scrubbed
2 tablespoons minced fresh cilantro
1 tablespoon drained capers

1. In spice mill or mini-jar of blender, combine bay leaves, peppercorns, cinnamon stick, oregano, cloves, cumin and allspice; process to a coarse powder.
2. Transfer spice mixture to small saucepan; add vinegar, juice and $^1/_4$ cup water. Bring liquid to a boil; reduce heat to low. Simmer, covered, 10 minutes. Remove from heat; let stand at least 2 hours. Strain; discard solids.
3. On paper plate or sheet of wax paper, coat one side of each piece of fish with flour.
4. In medium nonstick skillet, heat oil; add fish, flour-side down. Cook over medium-high heat, 1 minute, until golden brown. Turn fish over; cook 1 minute longer, until fish flakes easily when tested with fork. Transfer fish to serving platter, flour-side up; keep warm.
5. In same skillet, cook onions and carrots over medium heat, stirring frequently, 5 minutes, until onions are softened. Add chile peppers and garlic; cook, stirring frequently, 2 minutes longer.
6. Add strained spice liquid to vegetable mixture; bring liquid to a boil. Reduce heat to low; simmer 3 minutes, until carrots are tender-crisp.

7. Add oysters to vegetable mixture; cook, covered, 1–2 minutes, until oysters open.* With slotted spoon, arrange oysters and vegetables on platter with fish; do not remove skillet from heat.

8. Bring liquid in skillet to a boil; cook until liquid is reduced in volume to about $^1/_2$ cup. Pour liquid over fish and vegetables; sprinkle with cilantro and capers. Serve hot or refrigerate, covered, 1 hour.

Each serving provides: $^1/_4$ Fat, $1^1/_4$ Vegetables, 1 Protein, 5 Optional Calories

Per serving: 127 Calories, 3 g Total Fat, 0 g Saturated Fat, 29 mg Cholesterol, 111 mg Sodium, 16 g Total Carbohydrate, 2 g Dietary Fiber, 12 g Protein, 2 mg Calcium

*Discard any oysters that do not open.

VARIATION:

Fish and Mussel Escabeche: Substitute 16 large mussels in the shell, scrubbed and bearded, for the oysters.

Per serving: 132 Calories, 2 g Total Fat, 0 g Saturated Fat, 21 mg Cholesterol, 160 mg Sodium, 16 g Total Carbohydrate, 2 g Dietary Fiber, 13 g Protein, 54 mg Calcium

FISH WITH TOASTED GARLIC AND LIME

This exquisitely garlicky dish is the perfect centerpiece for a special dinner. Serve it with Green Rice with Peas (see page 135) and grilled tomatoes.

Makes 4 servings

¹/₄ cup fresh lime juice
¹/₂ teaspoon salt
Four 5-ounce catfish or grouper fillets, each ¹/₂" thick
1 tablespoon unsalted margarine
2 teaspoons corn oil
8 large garlic cloves, sliced
3 tablespoons all-purpose flour

¹/₄ teaspoon freshly ground black pepper
¹/₂ fluid ounce (1 tablespoon) dry white wine
2 tablespoons minced fresh cilantro
Lime slices, to garnish

1. To prepare marinade, in gallon-size sealable plastic bag, combine 3 tablespoons of the juice and ¹/₄ teaspoon of the salt; add fish. Seal bag, squeezing out air; turn to coat. Refrigerate 1 hour, turning bag occasionally.
2. Drain and rinse fish, then pat dry with paper towels.
3. In large nonstick skillet, heat together margarine and oil; add garlic. Cook over low heat; stirring constantly, 5 minutes, until golden brown (do not burn). Remove skillet from heat. With slotted spoon, transfer garlic to small bowl; set aside.
4. On paper plate or sheet of wax paper, combine flour, pepper and remaining ¹/₄ teaspoon salt; coat one side of each fillet with flour mixture.
5. In same skillet, cook fish, flour-side down, over medium heat, 3–4 minutes, until golden brown. Turn fillets over; cook 3 minutes longer, until fish flakes easily when tested with fork. Transfer fillets to serving platter; keep warm.
6. Add wine, cilantro, reserved garlic and remaining 1 tablespoon juice to skillet; cook over medium high heat, stirring constantly, 1–2 minutes, until most of liquid has evaporated. Spoon wine mixture over fish; garnish with lime slices.

Each serving (1 fish fillet) provides: 1^1/$_4$ Fats, 2 Proteins, ^{1}/$_4$ Bread, 5 Optional Calories

Per serving: 264 Calories, 15 g Total Fat, 3 g Saturated Fat, 47 mg Cholesterol, 256 mg Sodium, 8 g Total Carbohydrate, 0 g Dietary Fiber, 22 g Protein, 19 mg Calcium

VARIATION:

Buttery Fish with Toasted Garlic and Lime: Substitute 1 tablespoon sweet butter for the margarine; reduce Fat Selections to ^{1}/$_2$ and increase Optional Calories to 30.

Per serving: 264 Calories, 15 g Total Fat, 4 g Saturated Fat, 55 mg Cholesterol, 257 mg Sodium, 8 g Total Carbohydrate, 0 g Dietary Fiber, 22 g Protein, 19 mg Calcium

FISH GRILLED IN CORN HUSKS

Makes 4 servings

2 large garlic cloves, roasted
  and peeled (see page viii for
  roasting technique)
2 teaspoons pureed canned
  chipotle peppers in adobo
  sauce (see page vi for
  ingredient information)
1 teaspoon cider vinegar
$^1/_4$ teaspoon powdered bay leaf
$^1/_4$ teaspoon dried oregano leaves
$^1/_4$ teaspoon dried thyme leaves
$^1/_4$ teaspoon ground cinnamon
Pinch ground cumin

Pinch freshly ground black
  pepper
Pinch ground cloves
1 pound 4 ounces catfish
  or grouper fillets, cut into
  16 equal pieces
12 large dried corn husks,
  prepared for wrapping
  (see page ix for preparation
  technique), or 24 fresh corn
  husks, soaked in hot water
  for 30 minutes
Lime wedges, to garnish

1. To prepare marinade, in small bowl, combine garlic, pureed peppers, vinegar, bay leaf, oregano, thyme, cinnamon, cumin, black pepper and cloves; with back of wooden spoon, mash together. Transfer mixture to gallon-size sealable plastic bag; add fish, tossing to coat. Seal bag, squeezing out air; refrigerate 2 hours, turning bag occasionally.
2. Preheat outdoor barbecue grill according to manufacturer's directions.
3. Place 4 prepared dried corn husks (or 4 overlapping pairs of fresh corn husks) on work surface; divide marinated fish evenly among husks. Fold opposite long sides over fish, then fold short ends over fish to enclose.
4. Place each packet on another husk (or pair of husks), with packet's short ends facing long ends of second husk; repeat folding procedure.
5. With remaining husks, repeat wrapping procedure one more time. Grill packets over hot coals, turning once, until charred on both sides. Carefully remove and discard charred outer husks. Place packets on serving platter; garnish with lime wedges.

Each serving (1 packet) provides: 2 Proteins

Per serving: 191 Calories, 10 g Total Fat, 2 g Saturated Fat, 47 mg Cholesterol, 84 mg Sodium, 2 g Total Carbohydrate, 0 g Dietary Fiber, 21 g Protein, 11 mg Calcium

SAVORY CILANTRO SALMON

This gorgeous entrée is perfect for delighting your guests or pampering yourself, and it's so easy to prepare!

Makes 2 servings

1 1/2 cups fresh cilantro leaves
1 tablespoon fresh lime juice
1/2 teaspoon ground cumin
1/2 teaspoon salt
Dash hot red pepper sauce

Two 5-ounce salmon steaks
1 medium yellow bell pepper, seeded and sliced
1 medium red bell pepper, seeded and sliced

1. To prepare marinade, in food processor, combine cilantro, juice, cumin, salt, hot red pepper sauce and 1/4 cup water; purée until smooth.
2. Transfer marinade to gallon-size sealable plastic bag; add salmon. Seal bag, squeezing out air; turn to coat salmon. Refrigerate 1 hour, turning bag occasionally.
3. Preheat oven to 400°F. Spray 9" square baking dish with nonstick cooking spray.
4. Arrange pepper slices in a single layer in prepared pan; bake 20 minutes, turning peppers once.
5. Drain salmon; discard marinade. Place salmon on top of pepper slices; bake, turning salmon once, 12–14 minutes, until fish flakes easily when tested with fork.

Each serving (1 salmon steak + 1/2 of the pepper slices) provides:
2 Vegetables, 3 Proteins

Per serving: 236 Calories, 12 g Total Fat, 3 g Saturated Fat, 75 mg Cholesterol, 198 mg Sodium, 7 g Total Carbohydrate, 1 g Dietary Fiber, 24 g Protein, 43 mg Calcium

SALMON-MACKEREL SEVICHE

There are many versions of seviche, the cool, fresh-tasting salad that uses citrus juice, rather than heat, to "cook" fish and seafood. It makes an elegant first course or a light main course for a summer luncheon. For the best flavor, as well as to ensure food safety, be sure the fish is impeccably fresh!

Makes 4 servings

8 ounces mackerel or salmon
fillet, cut into 1/2" pieces
1/2 cup fresh lime juice
1 medium tomato, diced
1 medium jalapeño pepper,
seeded, deveined and minced
(see page v)
1/2 cup minced onion
1/4 cup tomato juice
10 small or 6 large green olives,
pitted and chopped

1 tablespoon minced fresh
cilantro
1 tablespoon olive oil
1/2 teaspoon dried oregano leaves
1/2 teaspoon granulated sugar
1/4 teaspoon salt
4 lettuce leaves
Lime slices and fresh cilantro
sprigs, to garnish

1. In medium nonreactive bowl,* combine fish and lime juice; toss to coat thoroughly. Place sheet of plastic wrap directly on surface of fish mixture to cover completely; refrigerate at least 5 hours or overnight.
2. Drain fish; discard liquid. Return fish to bowl. Add tomato, pepper, onion, tomato juice, olives, minced cilantro, oil, oregano, sugar and salt to fish; toss to combine. Refrigerate, covered, 1 hour.
3. Line serving platter with lettuce leaves. Top lettuce with fish mixture; garnish with lime slices and cilantro sprigs.

Each serving (3/4 cup) provides: 1 Fat, 1 1/2 Vegetables, 2 Proteins

Per serving: 180 Calories, 12 g Total Fat, 2 g Saturated Fat, 40 mg Cholesterol, 418 mg Sodium, 6 g Total Carbohydrate, 1 g Dietary Fiber, 12 g Protein, 30 mg Calcium

*It's best to marinate in bowls made of nonreactive material, such as glass, stainless steel or ceramic; ingredients such as lime juice may react with other materials, causing color and flavor changes in foods.

SHRIMP WITH GARLIC AND SPINACH

Serve this highly flavored shrimp dish with warm tortillas to sop up the sauce.

Makes 4 servings

1 teaspoon olive oil
$^1/_2$ cup coarsely chopped onion
4 large garlic cloves, coarsely
  chopped
2 medium poblano peppers,
  roasted, peeled, seeded and
  coarsely chopped (see page vi;
  see page ix for roasting
  technique)
$^1/_2$ cup tomato purée

1 teaspoon pureed canned
  chipotle peppers in adobo
  sauce (see page vi for
  ingredient information)
$^1/_2$ teaspoon granulated sugar
16 jumbo shrimp, brined, then
  peeled and deveined (see page
  viii for brining technique)*
1 cup cooked chopped spinach,
  squeezed dry

1. In medium nonstick skillet, heat oil; add onion. Cook over medium heat, stirring frequently, 8–10 minutes, until lightly browned. Stir in garlic; cook, stirring frequently, 2 minutes longer.
2. Transfer onion mixture to food processor or blender. Add roasted peppers, tomato purée, pureed peppers and sugar; purée until smooth.
3. Return mixture to skillet; cook over high heat, stirring constantly, 2 minutes, until slightly thickened. Reduce heat to low; add shrimp. Cook, stirring frequently, 2 minutes, until shrimp turn pink. Stir in spinach; cook, stirring constantly, 30 seconds, until heated through.

Each serving provides: 2 Vegetables, 2 Proteins, 10 Optional Calories

Per serving: 194 Calories, 4 g Total Fat, 0 g Saturated Fat, 172 mg Cholesterol, 650 mg Sodium, 14 g Total Carbohydrate, 4 g Dietary Fiber, 28 g Protein, 206 mg Calcium

* *One jumbo shrimp will yield about 1 ounce cooked, peeled and deveined shrimp.*

SPICY SHRIMP WITH BLACK BEAN SALSA

Beans are a Mexican staple and can be prepared in ways almost too numerous to count. Here we've combined them with colorful vegetables and fiery jalapeño pepper to make a marvelous salsa for shrimp.

Makes 4 servings

Salsa:

12 ounces drained cooked black beans

1 cup cubed yellow or green bell pepper

1 medium jalapeño pepper, seeded, deveined and minced (see page v)

$^1/_2$ cup chopped red onion

$^1/_4$ cup chopped celery

$^1/_4$ cup chopped fresh cilantro

1 garlic clove, crushed

2 tablespoons fresh lime juice

2 teaspoons olive or vegetable oil

Shrimp:

24 medium shrimp, peeled and deveined

$^1/_2$ fluid ounce (1 tablespoon) dry sherry

$1^1/_2$ teaspoons mild or hot chili powder

1 garlic clove, crushed

$^1/_2$ teaspoon ground cumin

$^1/_4$ teaspoon salt

2 teaspoons olive or vegetable oil

1. To prepare salsa, in medium bowl, combine beans, bell pepper, jalapeño pepper, onion, celery, cilantro, garlic, juice and oil; let stand, covered, until flavors are blended.
2. To prepare shrimp, in separate medium bowl, combine shrimp, sherry, chili powder, garlic, cumin and salt, tossing to coat.
3. In large nonstick skillet, heat oil; add shrimp mixture. Cook, stirring frequently, 4 minutes, until shrimp turn pink. Transfer shrimp to serving platter; serve with salsa.

Each serving provides: 1 Fat, $1^1/_4$ Vegetables, 3 Proteins, 5 Optional Calories

Per serving: 273 Calories, 7 g Total Fat, 1 g Saturated Fat, 129 mg Cholesterol, 282 mg Sodium, 27 g Total Carbohydrate, 3 g Dietary Fiber, 26 g Protein, 89 mg Calcium

Mini Tostadas with Cilantro-Shrimp Topping

These tostadas are more elegant than most; buy frozen cooked shrimp to make the preparation even quicker and easier.

Makes 4 servings

Two 6" corn tortillas
1/4 medium avocado, peeled
1/2 medium pickled jalapeño pepper, seeded
2 tablespoons finely diced onion
1 tablespoon fresh lime juice
1/4 teaspoon salt
Pinch freshly ground black pepper

8 medium shrimp, cooked, peeled and deveined
1/4 cup diced tomato
2 tablespoons chopped fresh cilantro
2 ounces drained cooked black beans

1. Preheat oven to 350°F. Spray baking sheet with nonstick cooking spray.
2. With 2" round biscuit cutter or kitchen scissors, cut four 2" circles from each tortilla; cut remaining tortillas into bite-size pieces. Place circles and pieces in a single layer on baking sheet; bake, turning frequently, 8 minutes, until crisp and golden brown.
3. In medium bowl, combine avocado, jalapeño pepper, onion, juice, salt and black pepper; with fork, mash mixture together until smooth. Add shrimp, tomato and cilantro; toss gently to combine.
4. In small bowl, with fork, mash beans; spread an equal amount of mashed beans on each tortilla circle. Top evenly with shrimp mixture; serve with remaining crisp tortilla pieces.

Each serving (2 tostadas + 1/4 of the tortilla pieces) provides: 1/2 Fat, 1/4 Vegetable, 3/4 Protein, 1/2 Bread

Per serving: 103 Calories, 3 g Total Fat, 2 g Saturated Fat, 55 mg Cholesterol, 249 mg Sodium, 12 g Total Carbohydrate, 1 g Dietary Fiber, 8 g Protein, 42 mg Calcium

SCALLOP SEVICHE

This version of the classic seviche makes an elegant first course or light entrée. Add Bolillos (see page 146) or biscuits, and a voluptuous dessert like Coffee Flan with Chocolate Sauce (see page 170) or Pay de Queso (see page 172), for a cooling summer luncheon.

Makes 4 servings

15 ounces bay scallops
$^{1}/_{2}$ cup fresh lemon juice
1 medium cucumber, pared, seeded and diced
1 teaspoon coarse (kosher) salt
1 medium tomato, finely diced
1 medium pickled jalapeño pepper, seeded and sliced (reserve 1 tablespoon juice)

$^{1}/_{4}$ cup sliced scallions (white portion with some green)
2 tablespoons minced fresh cilantro
4 lettuce leaves
Lemon slices, to garnish

1. In medium nonreactive bowl,* combine scallops and lemon juice; toss to coat thoroughly. Place sheet of plastic wrap directly on surface of scallop mixture to cover completely; refrigerate at least 5 hours or overnight.
2. While scallops are marinating, place cucumber in colander. Sprinkle with salt; toss to combine. Let cucumber mixture stand 2 hours. Rinse cucumber mixture under cold running water; let drain thoroughly.
3. Drain scallops; discard liquid. Return scallops to bowl. Add drained cucumber, tomato, pepper and reserved juice, scallions and cilantro; toss to combine. Refrigerate, covered, 1 hour.
4. Line serving platter with lettuce leaves. Top lettuce with scallop mixture; garnish with lemon slices.

Each serving (1 cup) provides: $1^{3}/_{4}$ Vegetables, $1^{1}/_{2}$ Proteins

Per serving: 112 Calories, 1 g Total Fat, 0 g Saturated Fat, 35 mg Cholesterol, 350 mg Sodium, 7 g Total Carbohydrate, 1 g Dietary Fiber, 19 g Protein, 45 mg Calcium

* *It's best to marinate in bowls made of nonreactive material, such as glass, stainless steel or ceramic; ingredients such as lemon juice may react with other materials, causing color and flavor changes in foods.*

BROILED SHARK STEAKS WITH ROAST PEPPER CREAM

You can grill these steaks outdoors if you like; add Potato and Pepper Salad (see page 120) and some sliced tomatoes for a lavish summer barbecue.

Makes 4 servings

Roast Pepper Cream:
2 servings ($^1/_4$ cup) Sweet
 and Hot Pepper Purée
 (see page 162)
1 tablespoon nonfat sour cream
$1^1/_2$ teaspoons plain nonfat
 yogurt
2 teaspoons fresh lime juice

Fish:
2 tablespoons fresh lime juice
$^1/_2$ teaspoon salt
Four 5-ounce skinless boneless
 shark steaks, each 1" thick
1 teaspoon olive oil
Lime wedges, to garnish

1. To prepare Roast Pepper Cream, in small bowl, combine Sweet and Hot Pepper Purée, sour cream, yogurt and juice; cover and refrigerate, 30 minutes, until flavors are blended.
2. To prepare fish, in gallon-size sealable plastic bag, combine juice and salt; add fish. Seal bag, squeezing out air; turn to coat. Refrigerate 1 hour, turning bag occasionally.
3. Preheat broiler. Spray rack in broiler pan with nonstick cooking spray.
4. Drain and rinse fish; pat dry with paper towels. Rub fish evenly with oil.
5. Place fish on prepared rack; broil 4" from heat, 3–5 minutes, until lightly charred. Turn fish over; broil 2–3 minutes longer, until fish flakes easily when tested with fork.
6. Transfer fish to serving platter. Stir pan juices into Roast Pepper Cream; serve fish with sauce and garnished with lime wedges.

Each serving (1 steak + $1^1/_2$ tablespoons sauce) provides: $^1/_4$ Fat, $^1/_2$ Vegetable, 2 Proteins, 5 Optional Calories

Per serving: 209 Calories, 8 g Total Fat, 1 g Saturated Fat, 72 mg Cholesterol, 393 mg Sodium, 3 g Total Carbohydrate, 0 g Dietary Fiber, 30 g Protein, 62 mg Calcium

CALAMARES EN SU TINTA (SQUID IN ITS OWN INK)

You'll find a dish similar to this in Spain and in Italy too. The squid ink darkens and flavors the sauce deliciously. For an elegant dinner, serve it on a bed of white rice with a light salad and a glass of red wine.

Makes 4 servings

1 pound 4 ounces small cleaned squid (reserve 2 teaspoons ink)*
2 fluid ounces ($^1/_4$ cup) dry red wine
2 teaspoons olive oil
$^1/_2$ cup finely chopped onion
$^1/_4$ cup minced green bell pepper
3 garlic cloves, crushed

1 medium tomato, halved and roasted (see page viii for roasting technique)
1 tablespoon minced fresh flat-leaf parsley
$^1/_2$ teaspoon granulated sugar
1 cup clam juice
1 bay leaf

1. Cut squid into rings and cut tentacles in half crosswise; set aside.
2. In small bowl, combine ink and wine; set aside.
3. In medium nonstick skillet, heat oil; add onion, bell pepper and garlic. Cook over medium heat, stirring frequently, 3 minutes, until onion is softened.
4. Transfer onion mixture to food processor or blender. Add tomato, parsley and sugar; purée until smooth.
5. Return mixture to skillet; stir in juice, bay leaf and ink mixture. Bring mixture to a boil; cook, stirring constantly, 3–5 minutes, until mixture is reduced and thickened. Reduce heat to low; add squid. Simmer 5 minutes, until squid is opaque. Remove and discard bay leaf.

Each serving (1 cup) provides: $^1/_2$ Fat, 1 Vegetable, 2 Proteins, 15 Optional Calories

Per serving (does not include ink; data not available): 189 Calories, 4 g Total Fat, 1 g Saturated Fat, 330 mg Cholesterol, 197 mg Sodium, 10 g Total Carbohydrate, 1 g Dietary Fiber, 23 g Protein, 68 mg Calcium

---

* *If your fishmonger can't provide squid ink, buy a large uncleaned squid along with the small ones. Hold body of large squid in one hand; pull tentacles out with the other. The ink sac is a small (1 × $^1/_{16}$") silvery sac in the gelatinous mass attached to the tentacles. Cut tentacles off just below eyes and set aside. Carefully remove ink sac and place in a strainer over a small bowl. Crush it with the back of a spoon to extract the ink; you'll need only 2 teaspoons of this intensely flavored liquid. Discard the squid or use it to make fish broth; large squid are sometimes tough.*

MEATLESS MAIN DISHES

Basic Mexican Omelet
Asparagus with Eggs and Cheese
Stuffed Poblano Peppers with Spiced Rice
Chiles Relleños
Vegetarian Empanadas with Yogurt Dipping Sauce
Eggplant and White Bean Tostadas
Pasta with Tomato-Molé Sauce
Mexican Pizza
Mexican Lasagna
Crustless Chile Quiche
Chilequiles
Mexicali Spuds

BASIC MEXICAN OMELET

This omelet combines whole eggs with egg substitute to keep the fat and cholesterol levels at bay. Light and luscious from the addition of ricotta cheese, it is delicious plain or topped with Ranchero Sauce (see page 158), warm or at room temperature.

Makes 4 servings

2 eggs
$^1/_2$ cup egg substitute
$^1/_2$ cup nonfat ricotta cheese
2 tablespoons minced fresh
   flat-leaf parsley or cilantro

$^1/_4$ teaspoon salt
$^1/_4$ teaspoon freshly ground black
   pepper

1. In medium bowl, with fork, beat eggs. Add egg substitute, cheese, parsley, salt and pepper; beat to combine.
2. Spray large nonstick skillet with nonstick cooking spray; heat. Add egg mixture; cook over medium heat, tilting to cover bottom of skillet, until bottom is set. Reduce heat to low; cook 3–4 minutes, until egg mixture is lightly browned on bottom. Remove from heat; let stand, covered, 5–7 minutes, until egg mixture is just set.
3. With spatula, carefully loosen edges of egg mixture; roll as tightly as possible, jelly-roll fashion. Transfer egg roll to serving platter; cut into 4 equal pieces.

Each serving (1 piece) provides: $1^1/_4$ Proteins, 10 Optional Calories

Per serving: 85 Calories, 3 g Total Fat, 1 g Saturated Fat, 109 mg Cholesterol, 247 mg Sodium, 3 g Total Carbohydrate, 0 g Dietary Fiber, 11 g Protein, 186 mg Calcium

VARIATION:

Vegetable Omelet: In small nonstick skillet, heat 1 teaspoon oil; add $^1/_2$ cup sliced onion, mushrooms, green or red bell pepper or spinach, or any combination of vegetables. Cook over medium heat, stirring frequently, until softened; spread over egg mixture before rolling. Add $^1/_4$ Fat and $^1/_4$ Vegetable Selections to Selection Information.

Per serving: 99 Calories, 4 g Total Fat, 1 g Saturated Fat, 109 mg Cholesterol, 249 mg Sodium, 4 g Total Carbohydrate, 0 g Dietary Fiber, 11 g Protein, 189 mg Calcium

ASPARAGUS WITH EGGS AND CHEESE

This is really an asparagus frittata. Serve it warm or cool as the centerpiece of a festive brunch.

Makes 4 servings

24 asparagus spears, cut into
  1" pieces
Boiling water
1 cup egg substitute
1¹/₂ ounces *queso fresco*,
  soft-textured pot cheese or
  soaked and drained feta cheese,
  crumbled (see page vii for
  soaking information)

¹/₂ teaspoon salt
¹/₄ teaspoon freshly ground
  black pepper
Pinch dried oregano leaves
Pinch ground nutmeg
2 teaspoons olive oil
¹/₂ cup minced onion
1 garlic clove, peeled

1. In large saucepan, cook asparagus in boiling water to cover 1–2 minutes, until tender-crisp. Drain; rinse with cold water to cool. Drain thoroughly; set aside.*
2. In medium bowl, combine egg substitute, cheese, salt, pepper, oregano and nutmeg; set aside.
3. In medium nonstick skillet, heat oil; add onion, garlic and reserved asparagus. Cook over medium heat, stirring frequently, 10 minutes, until asparagus are tender. Remove and discard garlic.
4. Add egg substitute mixture to asparagus mixture; stir quickly to combine. Reduce heat to low; cook 5–10 minutes, until mixture is set around edges and golden brown on bottom. Remove from heat; let stand, covered, 10 minutes, until mixture is just set. Cut into quarters; serve warm or at room temperature.

Each serving (1 quarter) provides: ¹/₂ Fat, 1¹/₄ Vegetables; 1¹/₂ Proteins

Per serving: 112 Calories, 5 g Total Fat, 2 g Saturated Fat, 8 mg Cholesterol, 451 mg Sodium, 6 g Total Carbohydrate, 1 g Dietary Fiber, 11 g Protein, 103 mg Calcium

* *If asparagus are less than ¹/₄" thick, omit this step.*

STUFFED POBLANO PEPPERS WITH SPICED RICE

Makes 4 servings

1 medium dried ancho pepper,
  seeded (see page ix for
  preparation technique)
Boiling water
2 teaspoons vegetable oil
1 cup chopped onions
1 garlic clove, minced
6 ounces uncooked regular (not
  converted) long-grain rice
One 2" piece cinnamon stick
$^1/_4$ teaspoon ground cloves
3 tablespoons dried currants

1 teaspoon grated orange zest*
$^3/_4$ teaspoon salt
2 tablespoons chopped fresh
  flat-leaf parsley
1 tablespoon fresh orange juice
$^1/_4$ teaspoon freshly ground black
  pepper
4 medium smooth-skinned
  poblano peppers, roasted,
  peeled, halved and seeded
  (see page vi; see page ix
  for roasting technique)

1. Place ancho pepper in small bowl; add boiling water to cover. Let stand 20 minutes; drain. Finely chop pepper.
2. Preheat oven to 350°F.
3. In medium saucepan, heat oil; add onions, garlic and ancho pepper. Cook, stirring frequently, 8 minutes, until onions are tender. Add rice, cinnamon stick and cloves; stir to coat. Stir in currants, zest, salt and $1^1/_4$ cups water; bring liquid to a boil. Reduce heat to low; simmer, covered, 20 minutes, until rice is tender and liquid is absorbed.
4. Add parsley, juice and black pepper to rice mixture; stir to combine.
5. Fill poblano halves with an equal amount of rice mixture. Place stuffed peppers in shallow baking dish; add 2 tablespoons water to dish. Bake, covered, 30 minutes, until heated throughout and very tender. Remove cover; bake 15 minutes longer, until lightly browned.

Each serving (2 stuffed pepper halves) provides: $^1/_2$ Fat, $^1/_4$ Fruit, $1^3/_4$ Vegetables, $1^1/_2$ Breads, 10 Optional Calories

Per serving: 251 Calories, 3 g Total Fat, 0 g Saturated Fat, 0 mg Cholesterol, 422 mg Sodium, 51 g Total Carbohydrate, 2 g Dietary Fiber, 6 g Protein, 53 mg Calcium

* *The zest of the orange is the peel without any of the pith (white membrane). To remove zest from orange, use a zester or the side of a vegetable grater.*

CHILES RELLEÑOS

This classic Mexican dish is easy to prepare and makes a great dish for your next fiesta.

Makes 4 servings

4 large smooth-skinned poblano peppers, roasted and peeled (see page vi; see page ix for roasting technique)

$^2/_3$ cup nonfat ricotta cheese

$2^1/_4$ ounces part-skim mozzarella cheese, shredded

$^1/_2$ cup finely chopped scallions (white portion with some green)

2 teaspoons corn oil

1. Preheat oven to 350°F. Spray baking sheet with nonstick cooking spray.
2. To prepare peppers, carefully slit open lengthwise; remove and discard seeds.
3. In small bowl, combine ricotta and mozzarella cheeses and scallions; shape into 4 bullet-shaped logs.
4. Insert 1 log into each prepared pepper; fold sides of peppers over filling to enclose. Place stuffed peppers, seam-side down, in a single layer, on prepared baking sheet; brush evenly with oil. Bake 7–10 minutes, until cheese is melted; serve immediately.

Each serving (1 stuffed pepper) provides: $^1/_2$ Fat, $1^3/_4$ Vegetables, $1^1/_4$ Proteins

Per serving: 131 Calories, 11 g Total Fat, 2 g Saturated Fat, 13 mg Cholesterol, 121 mg Sodium, 11 g Total Carbohydrate, 1 g Dietary Fiber, 12 g Protein, 337 mg Calcium

VEGETARIAN EMPANADAS WITH YOGURT DIPPING SAUCE

Empanadas seem like a great deal of work, but once they are made they can be frozen and baked just before serving. They can be eaten as an entrée, or double the recipe and serve half portions as great party hors d'oeuvres!

Makes 8 servings

Yogurt Dipping Sauce:
6 ounces yogurt cheese*
1 tablespoon fresh lime juice
1 garlic clove, minced
1 teaspoon salt
1 cup finely chopped fresh cilantro leaves

Dough:
2 tablespoons reduced-calorie tub margarine
1 tablespoon olive oil
$2^{1}/_{2}$ cups + 2 tablespoons all-purpose flour
1 teaspoon salt

Filling:
1 teaspoon olive oil
1 cup finely chopped onions
1 cup finely diced carrots
1 cup finely diced red bell pepper
1 cup finely diced zucchini
1 cup pared and finely diced eggplant
$^{1}/_{2}$ cup finely diced green bell pepper
1 medium jalapeño pepper, seeded, deveined and minced (see page v)
2 garlic cloves, minced
$^{1}/_{4}$ cup tomato purée
1 teaspoon chili powder
1 teaspoon ground cumin
$^{1}/_{2}$ teaspoon salt
$^{1}/_{4}$ cup finely chopped fresh flat-leaf parsley
2 tablespoons raisins, finely chopped
1 tablespoon + 1 teaspoon pignolias (pine nuts)

Glaze:
$^{1}/_{4}$ cup egg substitute

1. To prepare yogurt dipping sauce, in food processor or blender, combine yogurt cheese, juice, garlic and salt; purée until smooth. Add cilantro; with on-off motion, pulse processor just until combined (do not purée). Transfer mixture to serving bowl; refrigerate until chilled.

2. To prepare dough, in small saucepan, combine margarine, oil and ¹/₂ cup water; cook over medium-high heat, stirring occasionally, until margarine is melted. Remove from heat; set aside.

3. In clean food processor, combine 2¹/₂ cups of the flour and the salt. With machine on, slowly add margarine mixture; process until dough forms a ball and cleans sides of bowl. Wrap dough ball tightly in plastic wrap; let stand 15 minutes.

4. To prepare filling, in medium nonstick skillet, heat oil; add onions. Cook over medium-high heat, stirring frequently, 3 minutes, until softened. Add carrots, red bell pepper, zucchini, eggplant, green bell pepper, jalapeño pepper, garlic and ¹/₄ cup water; bring liquid to a boil. Reduce heat to medium; cook, stirring frequently, 7–10 minutes, until vegetables are soft.

5. Stir tomato purée, chili powder, cumin and salt into vegetable mixture; reduce heat to low. Cook, stirring frequently, 5 minutes. Add parsley, raisins and pignolias; stir to combine. Remove from heat; set aside.

6. Preheat oven to 350°F. Spray baking sheet with nonstick cooking spray.

7. Sprinkle work surface with remaining 2 tablespoons flour. With rolling pin, roll out dough on prepared surface to form a 20" square about ¹/₈" thick. With 6" round cookie cutter, cut thirty-two 6" circles from dough, occasionally rerolling scraps to use all of dough. Spoon an equal amount of filling onto bottom third of each dough circle. Moisten edges of dough with water; fold dough over filling to enclose, forming semicircles. With tines of fork, press firmly around curved edge of semicircle to seal. Transfer semicircles to prepared baking sheet; brush evenly with egg substitute. Bake 20 minutes, until lightly browned; serve warm with reserved yogurt dipping sauce.

Each main course serving (4 empanadas + 3 tablespoons sauce) provides:
1 Fat, 1³/₄ Vegetables, 1³/₄ Breads, 35 Optional Calories

Per serving: 248 Calories, 5 g Total Fat, 1 g Saturated Fat, 0 mg Cholesterol, 786 mg Sodium, 42 g Total Carbohydrate, 3 g Dietary Fiber, 8 g Protein, 94 mg Calcium

* To prepare yogurt cheese, line a colander with cheesecloth; place in deep bowl. Spoon 1¹/₂ cups plain nonfat yogurt (without gelatin or other additives) into colander; refrigerate, covered, at least 5 hours or overnight. Discard accumulated liquid. Makes about ³/₄ cup.

EGGPLANT AND WHITE BEAN TOSTADAS

Tostadas are quick and easy to make and are a delicious way to use leftovers. Experiment using different vegetables to create your own favorite.

Makes 4 servings

4 ounces drained cooked white kidney (cannellini) beans
$^1/_4$ cup plain nonfat yogurt
1 tablespoon fresh lime juice
2 garlic cloves, minced
$^3/_4$ teaspoon salt
Dash hot red pepper sauce
1 teaspoon olive oil
$^1/_2$ cup thinly sliced onion
$^1/_2$ cup pared and julienned eggplant

$^1/_2$ medium red bell pepper, seeded and julienned
1 tablespoon red wine vinegar
$^1/_2$ teaspoon mild or hot chili powder
$^1/_2$ teaspoon ground cumin
Four 6" corn tortillas
$^1/_2$ cup shredded carrot
$^1/_4$ cup chopped fresh cilantro

1. In food processor, combine beans, yogurt, juice, garlic, $^1/_2$ teaspoon of the salt and the hot pepper sauce; with on-off motion, pulse processor until mixture is combined but still lumpy (do not overprocess). Set aside.*
2. In medium nonstick skillet, heat oil; add onion. Cook over medium-high heat, stirring frequently, 3 minutes, until softened. Add eggplant and bell pepper; cook, stirring frequently, 5 minutes longer, until vegetables are tender.
3. Add vinegar, chili powder, cumin and remaining $^1/_4$ teaspoon salt to vegetable mixture; reduce heat to medium. Cook, stirring frequently, 7 minutes, until flavors are blended.†
4. Preheat oven to 450°F. Spray baking sheet with nonstick cooking spray.
5. Place tortillas in a single layer on prepared baking sheet; bake 5–7 minutes, until lightly browned and crisp. Top each tortilla with an equal amount of bean mixture, then vegetable mixture; sprinkle each with 2 tablespoons carrot and 1 tablespoon cilantro.

Each serving (1 tostada) provides: $^1/_4$ Fat, 1 Vegetable, $^1/_2$ Protein, 1 Bread, 10 Optional Calories

Per serving: 136 Calories, 2 g Total Fat, 0 g Saturated Fat, 0 mg Cholesterol, 476 mg Sodium, 25 g Total Carbohydrate, 4 g Dietary Fiber, 5 g Protein, 102 mg Calcium

* Recipe may be prepared ahead up to this point; refrigerate, covered, up to 2 days.

† Recipe may be prepared ahead up to this point; refrigerate, covered, up to one day.

PASTA WITH TOMATO-MOLÉ SAUCE

This is an unusual and delicious way to serve spaghetti.

Makes 4 servings

1 medium dried ancho pepper, seeded (see page vi for preparation technique)
$^1/_2$ cup boiling water
2 teaspoons vegetable oil
1 cup chopped onions
2 garlic cloves, minced
$^1/_4$ teaspoon ground cumin
Pinch ground cinnamon

3 tablespoons tomato paste
$^1/_8$ ounce ($^1/_8$ square) unsweetened chocolate
$^1/_2$ cup diced tomato
$^1/_2$ teaspoon salt
6 ounces spaghetti, cooked and drained
2 tablespoons chopped fresh flat-leaf parsley

1. To prepare tomato-molé sauce, in small bowl, combine pepper and water; let stand 20 minutes. Drain pepper; reserve liquid. Finely chop pepper; set aside.
2. In large nonstick saucepan, heat oil; add onions and garlic. Cook over medium heat, stirring frequently, 8 minutes, until onions are tender. Add reserved chopped pepper; cook, stirring frequently, 3–4 minutes longer, until mixture is golden brown. Add cumin and cinnamon; cook, stirring constantly, 1 minute longer.
3. Add tomato paste and reserved liquid to onion mixture; bring liquid to a boil. Reduce heat to low; simmer 5 minutes. Add chocolate; stir until melted. Add tomato and salt; cook, stirring frequently, until mixture is heated through.
4. Place spaghetti in large serving bowl; top with sauce, then sprinkle with parsley.

Each serving (1 cup spaghetti + 1 cup sauce) provides: $^1/_2$ Fat, $^1/_2$ Vegetable, 2 Breads, 5 Optional Calories

Per serving: 228 Calories, 4 g Total Fat, 1 g Saturated Fat, 0 mg Cholesterol, 379 mg Sodium, 42 g Total Carbohydrate, 3 g Dietary Fiber, 7 g Protein, 35 mg Calcium

Mexican Pizza

This is a quick-to-fix dish for an impromptu supper or snack.

Makes 8 servings

Ten 6" corn tortillas

1 medium dried guajillo pepper, seeded (see page ix for preparation technique)

4 medium tomatoes, halved and roasted (see page viii for roasting technique)

2 large garlic cloves, roasted and peeled (see page viii for roasting technique)

2 teaspoons corn oil

2 cups sliced onions

2 medium poblano peppers, roasted, peeled, seeded and sliced (see page vi; see page ix for roasting technique)

1 1/2 ounces *queso fresco*, soft-textured pot cheese or soaked and drained feta cheese, crumbled (see page vii for soaking information)

1 1/2 ounces Monterey Jack cheese, shredded

1 tablespoon grated Romano cheese

2 tablespoons minced fresh cilantro

1/4 teaspoon dried oregano leaves

1. Preheat oven to 450°F. Spray 14" nonstick pizza pan with nonstick cooking spray.
2. Wrap tortillas in foil; bake 15 minutes, until heated and softened. Remove tortillas from oven; leave oven on.
3. Meanwhile, in medium nonstick skillet, toast guajillo pepper over medium heat, stirring constantly, 30 seconds, until fragrant; transfer to food processor or blender. Add tomatoes and garlic; set aside.
4. In same skillet, heat oil; add onions. Cook over medium heat 8–10 minutes, until lightly browned; remove from heat. Transfer 1/2 cup of the cooked onions to food processor with the tomatoes; remove remaining onions from skillet and set aside.
5. Purée tomato mixture until smooth; transfer to same skillet. Cook tomato mixture over high heat, stirring constantly, 4–5 minutes, until thickened.
6. Unwrap tortillas; arrange 7 tortillas in prepared pizza pan, close to edge and overlapping as necessary. Arrange remaining 3 tortillas in center of pan, overlapping as necessary, to cover entire pan. Spray tortillas lightly with nonstick cooking spray.

7. Spread tomato mixture over tortillas. Evenly arrange poblano peppers and reserved onions over tomato mixture; sprinkle evenly with *queso fresco*, Monterey Jack and Romano cheeses, cilantro and oregano. Bake 10–15 minutes, until edge is golden brown and cheese is bubbling. Cut into 8 wedges.

Each serving (1 wedge) provides: $^1/_4$ Fat, 2 Vegetables, $^1/_2$ Protein, $1^1/_4$ Breads, 5 Optional Calories

Per serving: 165 Calories, 6 g Total Fat, 2 g Saturated Fat, 10 mg Cholesterol, 134 mg Sodium, 24 g Total Carbohydrate, 3 g Dietary Fiber, 6 g Protein, 149 mg Calcium

VARIATIONS:

Olive-Topped Pizza: Slice 12 large or 20 small pimiento-stuffed green olives; evenly arrange on pizza before baking. Increase Fat Selection to $^1/_2$.

Per serving: 173 Calories, 7 g Total Fat, 2 g Saturated Fat, 10 mg Cholesterol, 304 mg Sodium, 25 g Total Carbohydrate, 4 g Dietary Fiber, 6 g Protein, 153 mg Calcium

Jalapeño Pizza: Seed, devein and slice 2 medium jalapeño peppers; evenly arrange on pizza before baking. Increase Vegetable Selections to $2^1/_4$.

Per serving: 167 Calories, 6 g Total Fat, 2 g Saturated Fat, 10 mg Cholesterol, 134 mg Sodium, 25 g Total Carbohydrate, 3 g Dietary Fiber, 6 g Protein, 150 mg Calcium

Mexican Lasagna

This Mexican twist on an Italian favorite is filling and fun! It makes a great buffet dish or family dinner.

Makes 8 servings

9 ounces uncooked lasagna
noodles (about 9 noodles)
4 servings (2 cups) Refried Beans
(see page 128)
2¹/₂ cups tomato sauce

8 servings (4 cups) Vegetable
Filling (see page 125)
6 ounces sharp cheddar cheese,
shredded

1. Preheat oven to 300°F.
2. In large pot of boiling water, cook noodles 9–11 minutes, until tender. Drain; place noodles in bowl of cold water. Set aside.
3. In medium bowl, combine Refried Beans and ¹/₄ cup water; stir until spreadable consistency, adding more water, 1 tablespoon at a time, if needed.
4. In 13×9" baking pan, spread ¹/₂ cup tomato sauce.
5. Removing noodles from water and patting dry as needed, top sauce with one third of the noodles, ¹/₂ cup sauce, half of the Vegetable Filling and 2 ounces of the cheese, spreading evenly; repeat layers. Top cheese with remaining noodles, sauce and cheese. Bake 45 minutes, until cheese is melted and sauce is bubbling. Remove from oven; let stand 10 minutes.

Each serving provides: ³/₄ Fat, 5 Vegetables, 2 Proteins, 1¹/₂ Breads, 5 Optional Calories

Per serving: 406 Calories, 12 g Total Fat, 5 g Saturated Fat, 22 mg Cholesterol, 745 mg Sodium, 59 g Total Carbohydrate, 7 g Dietary Fiber, 18 g Protein, 245 mg Calcium

CRUSTLESS CHILE QUICHE

You may expect French cuisine when you hear "quiche," but this one is purely south-of-the-border.

Makes 4 servings

4 eggs

3 tablespoons all-purpose flour

2 tablespoons + 2 teaspoons reduced-calorie tub margarine, melted

1 tablespoon Dijon-style mustard

$^1/_4$ teaspoon salt

Dash hot red pepper sauce

1 cup nonfat cottage cheese

$1^1/_2$ ounces Monterey Jack cheese, shredded

$^1/_4$ cup drained canned mild or hot chopped green chile peppers

$^1/_2$ medium red bell pepper, roasted, peeled, seeded and diced (see page ix for roasting technique)

1 tablespoon grated Parmesan cheese

1. Preheat oven to 350°F. Spray 9" pie plate with nonstick cooking spray.
2. In medium bowl, beat eggs lightly. With wire whisk, add flour, margarine, mustard, salt and hot red pepper sauce, blending to combine. Stir in cottage and Monterey Jack cheeses and chile and bell peppers.
3. Transfer egg mixture to prepared pie plate; sprinkle evenly with Parmesan cheese. Bake 20–30 minutes, until mixture is set and top is golden brown. Remove from oven; let stand 10 minutes.

Each serving provides: 1 Fat, $^1/_2$ Vegetable, 2 Proteins, $^1/_4$ Bread, 10 Optional Calories

Per serving: 230 Calories, 13 g Total Fat, 4 g Saturated Fat, 230 mg Cholesterol, 769 mg Sodium, 10 g Total Carbohydrate, 0 g Dietary Fiber, 17 g Protein, 156 mg Calcium

CHILEQUILES

Sort of a cross between nachos and pizza, chilequiles are crunchy, gooey and delicious. A great way to use leftovers, they make a wonderful first course, snack or entrée in a soup-and-something supper.

Makes 4 servings

Eight 6" corn tortillas, each cut
   into eighths
4 servings (1¹/₃ cups) Cooked
   Red Sauce (see page 160)
   or Cooked Green Sauce
   (see page 161)

One or more Toppings (see below)
1¹/₂ ounces Monterey Jack cheese,
   shredded
2 tablespoons nonfat sour cream
2 tablespoons plain nonfat yogurt

1. Preheat oven to 250°F. Spray 9" flameproof pie pan with nonstick cooking spray.
2. Place tortilla pieces in a single layer on large baking sheet; bake 1 hour, until tortillas are very crisp and dry. Remove from oven; set aside.
3. In large bowl, toss tortilla pieces with sauce; spread evenly in prepared pie pan. Sprinkle evenly with topping(s), then cheese. Bake, loosely covered, 20 minutes, until heated through and cheese is melted.
4. Preheat broiler.
5. Broil tortilla mixture 4" from heat, 1 minute, until cheese is lightly browned.
6. In small bowl, combine sour cream and yogurt; spoon onto tortilla mixture. Serve immediately.

Each serving (with Cooked Red Sauce; without toppings) provides:
   ¹/₄ Fat, 2 Vegetables, ¹/₂ Protein, 2 Breads, 15 Optional Calories

Per serving: 216 Calories, 7 g Total Fat, 2 g Saturated Fat, 11 mg Cholesterol, 464 mg Sodium, 34 g Total Carbohydrate, 5 g Dietary Fiber, 8 g Protein, 205 mg Calcium

Each serving (with Cooked Green Sauce; without toppings) provides:
   ¹/₄ Fat, 1³/₄ Vegetables, ¹/₂ Protein, 2 Breads, 15 Optional Calories

Per serving: 256 Calories, 8 g Total Fat, 2 g Saturated Fat, 11 mg Cholesterol, 451 mg Sodium, 39 g Total Carbohydrate, 3 g Dietary Fiber, 11 g Protein, 224 mg Calcium

TOPPINGS

1. 1 cup thinly sliced onions (Add ¹/₂ Vegetable Selection)

Per serving of onions: 15 Calories, 0 g Total Fat, 0 g Saturated Fat, 0 mg Cholesterol, 1 mg Sodium, 3 g Total Carbohydrate, 1 g Dietary Fiber, 0 g Protein, 8 mg Calcium

2. 2 medium poblano peppers, roasted, peeled, seeded and cut into strips (see page vi; see page ix for roasting technique) (Add ¹/₂ Vegetable Selection)

Per serving of peppers: 12 Calories, 0 g Total Fat, 0 g Saturated Fat, 0 mg Cholesterol, 2 mg Sodium, 3 g Total Carbohydrate, 0 g Dietary Fiber, 1 g Protein, 6 mg Calcium

3. 2 medium jalapeño peppers, seeded, deveined and thinly sliced (see page v) (Add ¹/₂ Vegetable Selection)

Per serving of peppers: 3 Calories, 0 g Total Fat, 0 g Saturated Fat, 0 mg Cholesterol, 0 mg Sodium, 1 g Total Carbohydrate, 0 g Dietary Fiber, 0 g Protein, 1 mg Calcium

4. 1 cup steamed chopped spinach or Swiss chard (Add ¹/₂ Vegetable Selection)

Per serving of spinach: 10 Calories, 0 g Total Fat, 0 g Saturated Fat, 0 mg Cholesterol, 32 mg Sodium, 2 g Total Carbohydrate, 1 g Dietary Fiber, 1 g Protein, 61 mg Calcium

Per serving of Swiss chard: 9 Calories, 0 g Total Fat, 0 g Saturated Fat, 0 mg Cholesterol, 79 mg Sodium, 2 g Total Carbohydrate, 0 g Dietary Fiber, 1 g Protein, 26 mg Calcium

5. 1¹/₂ ounces *queso fresco*, soft-textured pot cheese or soaked and drained feta cheese, crumbled (see page vii for soaking information) (Add ¹/₂ Protein Selection)

Per serving of cheese: 34 Calories, 3 g Total Fat, 2 g Saturated Fat, 8 mg Cholesterol, 75 mg Sodium, 0 g Total Carbohydrate, 0 g Dietary Fiber, 2 g Protein, 56 mg Calcium

MEXICALI SPUDS

Stuffed potatoes never had it so good!

Makes 4 servings

1 teaspoon vegetable oil
$^1/_2$ cup diced red or green bell
   pepper
$^1/_2$ teaspoon mild or hot chili
   powder
$^1/_4$ teaspoon ground cumin
4 ounces drained cooked
   chick-peas (garbanzo beans),
   red kidney beans or black beans

$^1/_2$ cup prepared mild or hot salsa
Four 4-ounce hot baked potatoes
3 ounces sharp cheddar cheese,
   shredded
2 tablespoons finely chopped
   onion

1. In small nonstick skillet, heat oil; add bell pepper. Cook over medium-high heat, stirring frequently, 5 minutes, until softened; reduce heat to low. Add chili powder and cumin; cook, stirring constantly, 2 minutes longer. Stir in beans and salsa; bring mixture to a boil. Reduce heat to low; simmer 5 minutes, until flavors are blended.
2. With sharp knife, cut lengthwise slit about 1" deep into top of each potato, beginning and ending about $^1/_2$" from ends; squeeze ends gently toward each other until potato opens at slit.
3. Spoon one quarter of the bean mixture over each potato; sprinkle evenly with cheese and onion.

Each serving (1 potato) provides: $^1/_4$ Fat, $^1/_2$ Vegetable, $1^1/_2$ Proteins, 1 Bread

Per serving with chick-peas: 283 Calories, 9 g Total Fat, 5 g Saturated Fat, 22 mg Cholesterol, 467 mg Sodium, 40 g Total Carbohydrate, 4 g Dietary Fiber, 11 g Protein, 183 mg Calcium

Per serving with kidney beans: 272 Calories, 9 g Total Fat, 5 g Saturated Fat, 22 mg Cholesterol, 465 mg Sodium, 39 g Total Carbohydrate, 4 g Dietary Fiber, 11 g Protein, 177 mg Calcium

Per serving with black beans: 273 Calories, 9 g Total Fat, 5 g Saturated Fat, 22 mg Cholesterol, 465 mg Sodium, 40 g Total Carbohydrate, 3 g Dietary Fiber, 11 g Protein, 176 mg Calcium

7

SALADS AND SIDE DISHES

Christmas Eve Salad
Cauliflower Salad with Chile Peppers
Potato and Pepper Salad
Tex-Mex Potato Salad
Spicy Warm Corn Salad
Jicama-Fruit Salad
Zucchini with Roast Peppers and Corn
Vegetable Filling
Chayote with Herbed Summer Squash
Pozole (Hominy Stew)
Refried Beans
Roast Peppers with Onions
Mushroom-Stuffed Ancho Peppers
Vegetable-Stuffed Ancho Peppers
Shiitake Mushrooms with Corn
Mexican Rice with Vegetables
Green Rice with Peas
Rice with Seasoned Cream
Arroz à la Poblana (Rice with Peppers, Corn and Plantain)
Mexican Polenta
Swiss Chard with Potatoes
Potato-Pepper Gratin

CHRISTMAS EVE SALAD

As its name suggests, try this pretty and bright-tasting salad at holiday time as the centerpiece of a brunch. Roasted fresh beets may be substituted for the canned; they have *much* more flavor and are *much* less messy to prepare than boiled ones.

Makes 4 servings

2 small oranges, peeled and sectioned
1 medium banana, peeled and sliced
1 small apple, cored and sliced
1 cup roasted* or drained canned sliced beets
$^1/_8$ medium pineapple, pared, cored, and diced, or $^1/_2$ cup drained canned pineapple chunks (no sugar added)

3 tablespoons fresh lemon juice
3 tablespoons plain nonfat yogurt
3 tablespoons pineapple juice
1 teaspoon honey
Seeds from $^1/_2$ large pomegranate
$^1/_2$ ounce unsalted dry-roasted peanuts

1. In large bowl, combine oranges, banana, apple, beets, pineapple and lemon juice, tossing gently; refrigerate, covered, 1 hour.
2. In small bowl, combine yogurt, pineapple juice and honey; refrigerate, covered, 1 hour.
3. Arrange fruit mixture on serving platter; top with yogurt mixture. Spoon pomegranate seeds over yogurt mixture; sprinkle with peanuts.

Each serving provides: $^1/_4$ Fat, $1^3/_4$ Fruits, $^1/_2$ Vegetable, 25 Optional Calories

Per serving with fresh pineapple: 151 Calories, 2 g Total Fat, 0 g Saturated Fat, 0 mg Cholesterol, 110 mg Sodium, 33 g Total Carbohydrate, 4 g Dietary Fiber, 3 g Protein, 66 mg Calcium

Per serving with canned pineapple: 159 Calories, 2 g Total Fat, 0 g Saturated Fat, 0 mg Cholesterol, 110 mg Sodium, 35 g Total Carbohydrate, 4 g Dietary Fiber, 3 g Protein, 69 mg Calcium

---

* ***To roast beets:*** *Preheat oven to 400° F. Line baking sheet with foil; spray with nonstick cooking spray. Trim 2 medium beets, but do not peel; wrap each in foil. Place beets on prepared baking sheet; bake 1 hour, until tender. Cool, then peel and slice.*

CAULIFLOWER SALAD WITH CHILE PEPPERS

For a change, try broccoli instead of cauliflower in this salad, or combine the two. It makes a fine first course or side dish.

Makes 4 servings

2 cups thinly sliced cauliflower
2 tablespoons vegetable broth
1 tablespoon cider vinegar
2 teaspoons olive oil
1 large garlic clove, roasted (see page viii for roasting technique)
$^1/_2$ teaspoon Dijon-style mustard
$^1/_4$ teaspoon salt
Pinch dried oregano leaves
2 medium poblano peppers, roasted, peeled, seeded and sliced (see page vi; see page ix for roasting technique)

1 medium fresh hot chile pepper, roasted, peeled, seeded and sliced (see page ix for roasting technique)
$^1/_2$ medium red onion, thinly sliced
$^1/_2$ medium avocado, peeled, pitted and thinly sliced

1. In medium saucepan, bring 1 quart water to a rolling boil. Add cauliflower; cook 30 seconds, until tender-crisp. Drain, then rinse with cold water until cool; drain thoroughly.
2. Meanwhile, in small bowl or jar with tight-fitting lid, combine broth, vinegar, oil, garlic, mustard, salt and oregano; blend with small wire whisk, or cover and shake well.
3. In medium bowl, combine cooked cauliflower, poblano peppers, chile pepper and onion. Add broth mixture; toss to coat. Add avocado, toss gently to combine.

Each serving ($^3/_4$ cup) provides: $1^1/_2$ Fats, 2 Vegetables

Per serving: 110 Calories, 7 g Total Fat, 1 g Saturated Fat, 0 mg Cholesterol, 197 mg Sodium, 12 g Total Carbohydrate, 3 g Dietary Fiber, 3 g Protein, 35 mg Calcium

Potato and Pepper Salad

A change from the usual potato salad, this is a real crowd pleaser. It will make a casual meal special!

Makes 4 servings

15 ounces diced red potatoes (1" dice)

1 cup fresh or frozen corn kernels (see page x for fresh corn preparation technique)

2 tablespoons vegetable broth

2 tablespoons balsamic vinegar

1 tablespoon olive oil

1 large garlic clove, roasted (see page viii for roasting technique)

¹/₂ teaspoon salt

¹/₄ teaspoon freshly ground black pepper

2 medium poblano peppers, roasted, peeled, seeded and minced (see page vi; see page ix for roasting technique)

1 cup thinly sliced red onions

1 medium jalapeño pepper, seeded, deveined and sliced (see page v)

1 tablespoon cider vinegar

2 tablespoons minced fresh flat-leaf parsley

1. In medium saucepan, bring 3 cups water to a boil. Add potatoes; cook 5 minutes, until almost tender. Add corn; cook 2 minutes longer, until potatoes are just tender. Drain; transfer to large bowl.
2. Meanwhile, in small bowl or jar with tight-fitting lid, combine broth, balsamic vinegar, oil, garlic, salt and black pepper; blend with small wire whisk, or cover and shake well.
3. Add poblano peppers, onions, jalapeño pepper, cider vinegar and parsley to potato mixture; toss gently to combine. Add broth mixture; toss to coat. Let mixture cool to room temperature, tossing once or twice.

Each serving (1 cup) provides: ³/₄ Fat, 1¹/₄ Vegetables, 1¹/₄ Breads

Per serving: 184 Calories, 4 g Total Fat, 1 g Saturated Fat, 0 mg Cholesterol, 327 mg Sodium, 34 g Total Carbohydrate, 4 g Dietary Fiber, 5 g Protein, 25 mg Calcium

TEX-MEX POTATO SALAD

This creamy potato salad is easier than you ever thought possible with the help of the microwave oven. Add more jalapeño pepper if you like it especially hot.

Makes 4 servings

1 pound 4 ounces red potatoes, cut into $^3/_4$" cubes
1 cup cubed red or green bell pepper
1 cup sliced celery
1 medium jalapeño pepper, seeded, deveined and minced (see page v)

$^1/_4$ cup fat-free ranch salad dressing
1 teaspoon Worcestershire sauce
$^1/_2$ teaspoon paprika
$^1/_4$ teaspoon salt

1. In 2-quart microwave-safe casserole, combine potatoes and $^1/_2$ cup water; microwave on High (100% power), covered, 8–10 minutes, until potatoes are tender, stirring halfway through cooking. Drain; transfer potatoes to large bowl. Let cool slightly.
2. Add bell pepper, celery and jalapeño pepper to potatoes; toss to combine.
3. In small bowl, combine dressing, Worcestershire sauce, paprika, salt and 1 tablespoon water. Pour dressing mixture over potatoes; toss lightly to combine.

Each serving provides: $1^1/_4$ Vegetables, 1 Bread, 20 Optional Calories

Per serving: 155 Calories, 0 g Total Fat, 0 g Saturated Fat, 0 mg Cholesterol, 342 mg Sodium, 34 g Total Carbohydrate, 4 g Dietary Fiber, 3 g Protein, 16 mg Calcium

Spicy Warm Corn Salad

This brightly colored *picante* salad is different than expected, as it's served crisp and warm. Try it on a cool autumn day.

Makes 4 servings

2 cups drained cooked fresh or frozen corn kernels (see page x for fresh corn preparation technique)

1 medium red bell pepper, seeded and finely diced

3 tablespoons chopped fresh cilantro

2 teaspoons vegetable oil

1 ^{1}/$_2$ cups chopped red onions

2 medium jalapeño peppers, seeded, deveined and finely chopped (see page v)

2 garlic cloves, minced

1 tablespoon distilled white vinegar

^{1}/$_4$ teaspoon salt

Pinch freshly ground black pepper

1. In medium bowl, combine corn, bell pepper and cilantro; set aside.
2. In large nonstick skillet, heat oil; add onions, jalapeño peppers and garlic; cook over medium heat, stirring frequently, 8 minutes, until onions are tender. Add vinegar, salt and black pepper; stir to combine.
3. Add onion mixture to corn mixture; toss to combine. Serve immediately.

Each serving (^{3}/$_4$ cup) provides: ^{1}/$_2$ Fat, 1^3/$_4$ Vegetables, 1 Bread

Per serving: 144 Calories, 3 g Total Fat, 0 g Saturated Fat, 1 mg Cholesterol, 157 mg Sodium, 29 g Total Carbohydrate, 4 g Dietary Fiber, 4 g Protein, 25 mg Calcium

JICAMA-FRUIT SALAD

This peppery, sweet-tart salad is more a relish than a dessert. Serve it with broiled meat and poultry, or serve it as a refreshing first course.

Makes 8 servings

2 cups pared and diced jicama
(¹/₂" dice)

2 tablespoons grapefruit juice

2 tablespoons fresh lime juice

2 tablespoons fresh orange juice

1 teaspoon grated orange zest*

¹/₄ teaspoon ground red pepper,
or to taste

¹/₄ teaspoon freshly ground black
pepper, or to taste

¹/₄ teaspoon salt

2 small navel oranges, peeled and
sectioned

1 medium papaya or small
mango, peeled, seeded and
diced

1 small Granny Smith apple,
cored and diced

1 cup whole strawberries, sliced

2 tablespoons minced fresh
cilantro

1. In medium nonreactive bowl,† combine jicama, grapefruit juice, lime juice, orange juice and zest, red and black peppers and salt; refrigerate, covered, 1 hour.

2. Add oranges, papaya, apple, strawberries and cilantro to jicama mixture; toss to combine. Refrigerate, covered, tossing occasionally, 15 minutes, until flavors are blended.

Each serving (1 cup) provides: ³/₄ Fruit, ¹/₂ Vegetable, 5 Optional Calories

Per serving with papaya: 60 Calories, 0 g Total Fat, 0 g Saturated Fat, 0 mg Cholesterol, 71 mg Sodium, 15 g Total Carbohydrate, 2 g Dietary Fiber, 1 g Protein, 32 mg Calcium

Per serving with mango: 58 Calories, 0 g Total Fat, 0 g Saturated Fat, 0 mg Cholesterol, 70 mg Sodium, 14 g Total Carbohydrate, 2 g Dietary Fiber, 1 g Protein, 25 mg Calcium

* *The zest of the orange is the peel without any of the pith (white membrane). To remove zest from orange, use a zester or the side of a vegetable grater.*

†*It's best to marinate in bowls made of nonreactive material, such as glass, stainless steel or ceramic; ingredients such as citrus juices may react with other materials, causing color and flavor changes in foods.*

ZUCCHINI WITH ROAST PEPPERS AND CORN

Serve this creamy side dish with a simple broiled chicken or steak dinner, or make it the centerpiece of a light luncheon with a platter of sliced tomatoes and whole-wheat rolls.

Makes 4 servings

5 medium zucchini, diced ($^{1}/_{2}$" dice)

2 teaspoons salt

2 teaspoons corn oil

2 cups thinly sliced onions

1 cup fresh or frozen corn kernels (see page x for fresh corn preparation technique)

2 medium poblano peppers, roasted, peeled, seeded and sliced (see page vi; see page ix for roasting technique)

1 medium red bell pepper, roasted, peeled, seeded and sliced (see page ix for roasting technique)

1 cup evaporated skimmed milk

$^{1}/_{2}$ teaspoon salt

$^{1}/_{4}$ teaspoon freshly ground black pepper

$^{1}/_{4}$ cup nonfat sour cream

1 teaspoon cider vinegar

1. Place zucchini in colander. Sprinkle with salt; toss to combine. Let zucchini mixture stand 30 minutes. Rinse zucchini mixture under cold running water; let drain thoroughly, then pat dry with paper towels.
2. In large nonstick skillet, heat oil; add zucchini and onions. Cook over medium-high heat, stirring frequently, 8–10 minutes, until mixture is golden brown.
3. Add corn, poblano peppers, bell pepper, milk, salt and black pepper to vegetable mixture; stir to combine. Bring liquid to a boil over high heat; cook, stirring constantly, until liquid is reduced in volume by about half. Stir in sour cream and vinegar.

Each serving (1$^{1}/_{4}$ cups) provides: $^{1}/_{2}$ Milk, $^{1}/_{2}$ Fat, 4$^{1}/_{2}$ Vegetables, $^{1}/_{2}$ Bread, 10 Optional Calories

Per serving: 194 Calories, 3 g Total Fat, 0 g Saturated Fat, 3 mg Cholesterol, 654 mg Sodium, 34 g Total Carbohydrate, 4 g Dietary Fiber, 12 g Protein, 271 mg Calcium

VEGETABLE FILLING

This vibrant vegetable mélange is the perfect filling for enchiladas, burritos and tacos; or you can enjoy it as a side dish with meat, fish and poultry. For a unique meal, try it in Mexican Lasagna (see page 112).

Makes 4 servings

2 teaspoons vegetable oil
1¹/₂ cups thinly sliced onions
1¹/₄ cups julienned red bell pepper
1 medium jalapeño pepper, seeded, deveined and julienned (see page v)
1 garlic clove, minced

1¹/₂ cups halved and thinly sliced zucchini
1¹/₂ cups halved and thinly sliced yellow squash
¹/₄ teaspoon salt
¹/₄ teaspoon freshly ground black pepper

1. In large nonstick skillet, heat oil; add onions, bell pepper, jalapeño pepper and garlic. Cook over medium heat, stirring frequently, 8 minutes, until vegetables are tender.
2. Add zucchini, yellow squash, salt and black pepper to onion mixture; cook, covered, 10 minutes, until zucchini is tender-crisp.

Each serving (¹/₂ cup) provides: ¹/₂ Fat, 3¹/₄ Vegetables

Per serving: 70 Calories, 3 g Total Fat, 0 g Saturated Fat, 0 mg Cholesterol, 140 mg Sodium, 11 g Total Carbohydrate, 2 g Dietary Fiber, 2 g Protein, 36 mg Calcium

CHAYOTE WITH HERBED SUMMER SQUASH

Using the microwave may not be traditionally Mexican, but it sure makes preparing this side dish easy!

Makes 4 servings

Two 5-ounce chayotes, halved and seeded (see page vii for ingredient information)
1 cup coarsely chopped yellow squash
2 tablespoons chopped fresh flat-leaf parsley

2 teaspoons Dijon-style mustard
2 teaspoons olive oil
$^1/_2$ teaspoon dried thyme leaves
2 teaspoons grated Asiago or Parmesan cheese

1. In 2-quart microwave-safe casserole or on round platter, place chayote halves skin-side down; sprinkle with 2 tablespoons water. Microwave on High (100% power), covered, 6 minutes, until tender. Set aside to cool.
2. In small microwave-safe bowl, combine yellow squash, parsley, mustard, oil and thyme; microwave on High, covered, 1 minute.
3. Gently scoop pulp from cooled chayotes onto double layer of paper towels, leaving $^1/_4$" shells; reserve shells and let pulp drain.
4. Coarsely chop drained chayote pulp; stir into yellow squash mixture. Divide chayote mixture among reserved shells; arrange in same casserole. Microwave on High, uncovered, 2 minutes, until heated; sprinkle evenly with cheese.

Each serving (1 stuffed chayote shell) provides: $^1/_2$ Fat, $1^1/_2$ Vegetables, 5 Optional Calories

Per serving with Asiago cheese: 52 Calories, 3 g Total Fat, 1 g Saturated Fat, 1 mg Cholesterol, 78 mg Sodium, 5 g Total Carbohydrate, 0 g Dietary Fiber, 1 g Protein, 36 mg Calcium

Per serving with Parmesan cheese: 50 Calories, 3 g Total Fat, 0 g Saturated Fat, 0 mg Cholesterol, 80 mg Sodium, 5 g Total Carbohydrate, 0 g Dietary Fiber, 1 g Protein, 37 mg Calcium

POZOLE (HOMINY STEW)

Hominy is a hearty grain unknown to Europeans before they settled in the New World; dishes prepared with this grain are purely "western natives." Here, we've combined hominy with the essence of Mexican cuisine to create a warming, filling stew that's perfect on those cold winter nights.

Makes 4 servings

2 tablespoons shelled raw pumpkin seeds
4 medium tomatillos, husked and roasted (see page viii for roasting technique)
2 teaspoons corn oil
1 cup chopped onions
1 medium jalapeño pepper, seeded, deveined and minced (see page v)
2 large garlic cloves, minced
4 cups drained cooked whole hominy

2 cups low-sodium chicken broth
1/2 cup minced fennel leaves
2 tablespoons minced fresh epazote or flat-leaf parsley
1/2 teaspoon freshly ground black pepper
Pinch salt
1/2 cup finely chopped tomato
1/2 cup minced red onion or scallions (white portion with some green)
1/4 teaspoon dried oregano leaves
1 lime, cut into wedges

1. In large nonstick skillet, cook pumpkin seeds over medium-low heat, stirring constantly, 3–5 minutes, until popped and golden brown; transfer to food processor or blender. Add tomatillos; purée until smooth.
2. In same skillet, heat oil; add chopped onions. Cook over medium heat, stirring frequently, 8–10 minutes, until lightly browned. Add jalapeño pepper and garlic; cook, stirring frequently, 2 minutes longer.
3. Add hominy, broth, fennel, epazote, black pepper and salt to onion mixture; bring liquid to a boil. Reduce heat to low; simmer, stirring occasionally, 1 hour, until thickened and flavors are blended.
4. Meanwhile, in small bowl, combine tomato, red onion and oregano. Serve stew with tomato mixture and lime wedges.

Each serving (1 1/4 cups stew + 3 tablespoons tomato mixture) provides:
1/2 Fat, 2 Vegetables, 2 Breads, 35 Optional Calories

Per serving: 276 Calories, 7 g Total Fat, 1 g Saturated Fat, 0 mg Cholesterol, 125 mg Sodium, 55 g Total Carbohydrate, 7 g Dietary Fiber, 10 g Protein, 51 mg Calcium

REFRIED BEANS

Refried beans are a mealtime staple in Mexico; this lower-in-fat version will please your taste buds as well as your waistline.

Makes 4 servings

1 tablespoon vegetable oil	1 teaspoon ground cumin
1$^1/_2$ cups chopped onions	Pinch ground red pepper
3 garlic cloves, minced	1 pound drained cooked pinto
2 teaspoons mild or hot chili	beans
powder	

1. In large nonstick skillet, heat oil; add onions, garlic, chili powder, cumin and pepper. Cook over medium-low heat, stirring frequently, 8 minutes, until onions are tender.
2. Add beans, $^1/_4$ cup at a time, mashing and mixing with wooden spoon, until mixture is coarsely mashed, adding water, 1 teaspoon at a time, to keep mixture from sticking. Stir in additional water, 1 teaspoon at a time, until mixture is slightly creamy but still very firm.

Each serving ($^1/_2$ cup) provides: $^3/_4$ Fat, $^3/_4$ Vegetable, 2 Proteins

Per serving: 218 Calories, 4 g Total Fat, 1 g Saturated Fat, 0 mg Cholesterol, 18 mg Sodium, 36 g Total Carbohydrate, 6 g Dietary Fiber, 10 g Protein, 79 mg Calcium

ROAST PEPPERS WITH ONIONS

This hearty vegetable combo is delicious served as a relish with meat, fish and poultry. For variety, add your favorite green or starchy vegetable along with the broth to make an even more special vegetable dish.

Makes 4 servings

1 teaspoon corn or olive oil
1 cup thickly sliced onions
4 medium poblano peppers, roasted, peeled, seeded and sliced (see page vi; see page ix for roasting technique)
2 garlic cloves, crushed

$^1/_2$ cup vegetable or low-sodium chicken broth
$^1/_4$ teaspoon dried thyme leaves
$^1/_4$ teaspoon dried oregano leaves
1 bay leaf
Pinch salt

1. In medium nonstick skillet, heat oil; add onions. Cook over medium heat, stirring frequently, 8–10 minutes, until onions are lightly browned. Add peppers and garlic; cook, stirring frequently, 2 minutes longer.
2. Add broth, thyme, oregano, bay leaf and salt to onion mixture; bring liquid to a boil over high heat. Cook, stirring occasionally, until most of the liquid has evaporated. Remove and discard bay leaf; serve mixture hot or at room temperature.

Each serving (scant $^1/_2$ cup) provides: $^1/_4$ Fat, $1^1/_2$ Vegetables, 5 Optional Calories

Per serving with vegetable broth: 57 Calories, 1 g Total Fat, 0 g Saturated Fat, 0 mg Cholesterol, 166mg Sodium, 11 g Total Carbohydrate, 1 g Dietary Fiber, 2 g Protein, 31 mg Calcium

Per serving with chicken broth: 58 Calories, 1 g Total Fat, 0 g Saturated Fat, 0 mg Cholesterol, 56 mg Sodium, 11 g Total Carbohydrate, 1 g Dietary Fiber, 2 g Protein, 33 mg Calcium

MUSHROOM-STUFFED ANCHO PEPPERS

The ancho peppers combined with the mushrooms give this dish an almost meaty flavor. They can be prepared in the morning, refrigerated and just popped into the oven before serving.

Makes 4 servings

Peppers:

8 large dried ancho peppers
Boiling water
1 cup whole mushrooms, finely minced
1 ounce dried porcini mushrooms, soaked, drained and finely minced
2 teaspoons corn oil
$^1/_4$ cup minced onion

1 small garlic clove, crushed
2 tablespoons balsamic vinegar
4 ounces cooked red potatoes, pared and diced ($^1/_4$" dice)
1 tablespoon minced fresh flat-leaf parsley
Pinch salt
Pinch freshly ground black pepper

Tomato Broth:

4 medium tomatoes, halved and roasted (see page viii for roasting technique)
1 medium fresh hot chile pepper, roasted, peeled, seeded and coarsely chopped (see page v; see page ix for roasting technique)

2 large garlic cloves, roasted and peeled (see page viii for roasting technique)
$^1/_4$ cup vegetable broth

Topping:

1$^1/_2$ ounces *queso fresco,* soft-textured pot cheese or soaked and drained feta cheese, crumbled (see page vii for soaking information)

$^1/_4$ cup nonfat sour cream

1. To prepare peppers, place peppers in large bowl; add boiling water to cover (weigh peppers down with plate to keep submerged). Let stand 20–40 minutes, until very pliable.
2. Preheat oven to 375°F. Spray 10" glass pie plate or other shallow baking dish with nonstick cooking spray.

3. Drain peppers. Carefully slit peppers open lengthwise; remove and discard seeds. Rinse peppers; set aside.

4. Place mushrooms together on clean tea towel; twist and squeeze to extract as much liquid as possible.

5. In medium nonstick skillet, heat oil; add onion and mushrooms. Cook over medium-high heat, stirring frequently, 8–10 minutes, until onion is lightly browned and mixture is dry. Add garlic; cook, stirring frequently, 2 minutes longer. Add vinegar; cook, stirring constantly, until liquid has evaporated. Remove from heat; add potatoes, parsley, salt and pepper.

6. Carefully stuff each prepared pepper with an equal amount of mushroom mixture; fold sides of peppers over to enclose, securing with toothpicks if necessary. Place stuffed peppers, seam-side up, in a single layer, in prepared pie plate; set aside.

7. To prepare tomato broth, in food processor or blender, combine tomatoes, pepper and garlic; purée until smooth.

8. Place medium sieve over small bowl. Strain tomato mixture through sieve, pressing with back of wooden spoon; discard solids. Stir broth into tomato mixture; spoon around stuffed peppers.* Bake, tightly covered, 30 minutes.

9. Meanwhile, to prepare topping, in small bowl, combine cheese and sour cream; refrigerate, covered, until needed.

10. Remove toothpicks from peppers. Spoon topping over stuffed peppers; bake 5 minutes longer.

Each serving (2 stuffed peppers + $^1/_4$ of the broth and topping) provides:
$^1/_2$ Fat, $6^1/_4$ Vegetables, $^1/_2$ Protein, $^1/_4$ Bread, 10 Optional Calories

Per serving: 258 Calories, 11 g Total Fat, 3 g Saturated Fat, 8 mg Cholesterol, 211 mg Sodium, 40 g Total Carbohydrate, 3 g Dietary Fiber, 10 g Protein, 142 mg Calcium

* *Recipe may be prepared ahead up to this point; refrigerate stuffed peppers, covered, up to one day. Preheat oven about 15 minutes before baking; increase baking time to 40 minutes.*

VEGETABLE-STUFFED ANCHO PEPPERS

A wonderful side dish or hearty appetizer, these stuffed peppers are a definite change of pace.

Makes 4 servings

4 medium dried ancho peppers	$^1/_4$ teaspoon salt
Boiling water	Pinch freshly ground black pepper
2 teaspoons vegetable oil	$1^1/_2$ ounces extra-sharp cheddar
$^3/_4$ cup chopped onions	cheese, shredded
1 garlic clove, minced	2 tablespoons chopped fresh
1 cup diced red bell pepper	flat-leaf parsley
$1^1/_4$ cups diced zucchini	1 teaspoon distilled white vinegar

1. To prepare peppers, place peppers in large bowl; add boiling water to cover (weigh peppers down with plate to keep submerged). Let stand 20–40 minutes, until very pliable.

2. Preheat oven to 350°F. Spray shallow baking dish with nonstick cooking spray.

3. Drain peppers. Carefully slit peppers open lengthwise; remove and discard seeds. Rinse peppers; set aside.

4. In large nonstick skillet, heat oil; add onions and garlic. Cook over medium-high heat, stirring frequently, 4–5 minutes, until onions are translucent. Add bell pepper; cook, stirring frequently, 4–5 minutes longer, until bell pepper is softened. Add zucchini, salt and black pepper; cook, stirring frequently, 5 minutes longer, until zucchini is softened. Transfer vegetable mixture to medium bowl; let stand 5 minutes.

5. Add cheese, parsley and vinegar to vegetable mixture; stir to combine. Carefully stuff each prepared pepper with an equal amount of vegetable mixture; fold sides of peppers over to enclose, securing with toothpicks if necessary. Place stuffed peppers, seam-side up, in a single layer, in prepared dish; bake, covered, 20 minutes, until heated through.

Each serving (1 stuffed pepper) provides: $^1/_2$ Fat, $2^1/_2$ Vegetables, $^1/_2$ Protein

Per serving: 136 Calories, 9 g Total Fat, 3 g Saturated Fat, 11 mg Cholesterol, 209 mg Sodium, 14 g Total Carbohydrate, 1 g Dietary Fiber, 5 g Protein, 117 mg Calcium

SHIITAKE MUSHROOMS WITH CORN

When prepared with vegetable broth, this dish makes a delicious vegetarian first course for four; for a main course for two, simply double the serving size. Serve with warm tortillas to scoop up the savory morsels.

Makes 4 servings

2 teaspoons olive oil
1 cup finely chopped onions
$^1/_3$ cup finely chopped red bell
  pepper
3 cups sliced shiitake mushrooms
2 small garlic cloves, crushed
1 cup fresh or frozen corn kernels
  (see page x for fresh corn
  preparation technique)

$^1/_4$ cup low-sodium chicken broth
  or vegetable broth
$^1/_4$ teaspoon salt
1 tablespoon minced fresh
  epazote or flat-leaf parsley

1. In medium nonstick skillet, heat oil; add onions and bell pepper. Cook over medium heat, stirring frequently, 8–10 minutes, until onions are lightly browned. Add mushrooms and garlic to onion mixture; cook, stirring frequently, 5 minutes longer.
2. Stir corn, broth and salt into mushroom mixture; cook, covered, 5 minutes. Increase heat to high; cook, uncovered, stirring frequently, until most of the liquid has evaporated. Stir in epazote.

Each serving (scant $^3/_4$ cup) provides: $^1/_2$ Fat, $2^1/_4$ Vegetables, $^1/_2$ Bread

Per serving with chicken broth: 87 Calories, 3 g Total Fat, 0 g Saturated Fat, 0 mg Cholesterol, 153 mg Sodium, 14 g Total Carbohydrate, 3 g Dietary Fiber, 3 g Protein, 17 mg Calcium

Per serving with vegetable broth: 87 Calories, 3 g Total Fat, 0 g Saturated Fat, 0 mg Cholesterol, 207 mg Sodium, 14 g Total Carbohydrate, 3 g Dietary Fiber, 3 g Protein, 16 mg Calcium

MEXICAN RICE WITH VEGETABLES

A simple, home-style dish that is quick to prepare, this makes a good side dish or, with the addition of some cheese or sliced hard-cooked egg, a vegetarian entrée.

Makes 4 servings

2 teaspoons corn oil
6 ounces uncooked converted
 rice
$^1/_2$ cup chopped onion
$1^1/_2$ cups finely diced carrots
1 garlic clove, crushed

$1^1/_2$ cups stewed tomatoes, pureed
1 cup low-sodium chicken broth
$^1/_2$ teaspoon salt
$^1/_2$ cup frozen green peas
2 tablespoons minced fresh flat-leaf
 parsley

1. In medium saucepan, heat oil; add rice and onion. Cook over medium heat, stirring frequently, 8–10 minutes, until mixture is golden brown. Add carrots and garlic; cook, stirring constantly, 1 minute longer.
2. Add tomatoes, broth and salt to rice mixture; bring liquid to a boil, stirring frequently. Reduce heat to low; simmer, covered, 20 minutes, until most of the liquid is absorbed and rice is almost tender. Remove from heat; stir in peas. Let mixture stand, covered, 5–10 minutes, until all of the liquid is absorbed and rice is tender. Serve sprinkled with parsley.

Each serving ($1^1/_4$ cups) provides: $^1/_2$ Fat, $1^3/_4$ Vegetables, $1^3/_4$ Breads, 5 Optional Calories

Per serving: 250 Calories, 3 g Total Fat, 1 g Saturated Fat, 0 mg Cholesterol, 585 mg Sodium, 50 g Total Carbohydrate, 5 g Dietary Fiber, 6 g Protein, 88 mg Calcium

GREEN RICE WITH PEAS

This pretty side dish complements grilled or poached meat, fish and poultry.

Makes 4 servings

1¹/₂ cups low-sodium chicken broth

2 medium poblano peppers, roasted, peeled, seeded and chopped (see page vi; see page ix for roasting technique)

1 cup chopped romaine lettuce leaves

¹/₂ cup chopped onion

¹/₂ cup chopped celery

¹/₂ cup fresh cilantro sprigs

¹/₂ cup fresh flat-leaf parsley sprigs

1 large clove garlic, peeled

1 teaspoon corn oil

6 ounces uncooked converted rice

1 cup frozen green peas

8 fresh mint leaves

1 lemon wedge

Additional lemon wedges, to garnish

1. In medium saucepan, combine broth, peppers, lettuce, onion, celery, half the cilantro, half the parsley and the garlic; bring liquid to a boil. Reduce heat to low; simmer 10 minutes, until vegetables are tender.
2. Transfer broth mixture, in batches, to food processor or blender; purée until smooth. Set aside.
3. In medium nonstick skillet, heat oil; add rice. Cook over medium heat, stirring frequently, 4–7 minutes, until rice is lightly browned.
4. Slowly and carefully, add broth mixture to rice; bring liquid to a boil. Reduce heat to low; simmer 12–15 minutes, until almost all of the liquid is absorbed and rice is almost tender. Remove from heat; stir in peas. Let mixture stand, covered, 5–10 minutes, until all of the liquid is absorbed and rice is tender; transfer to serving bowl.
5. Finely chop together mint, remaining cilantro and remaining parsley; sprinkle rice mixture with chopped herbs and juice from 1 lemon wedge. Serve garnished with additional lemon wedges.

Each serving (1¹/₄ cups) provides: ¹/₄ Fat, 1¹/₂ Vegetables, 2 Breads, 10 Optional Calories

Per serving: 235 Calories, 3 g Total Fat, 1 g Saturated Fat, 0 mg Cholesterol, 106 mg Sodium, 47 g Total Carbohydrate, 4 g Dietary Fiber, 7 g Protein, 76 mg Calcium

RICE WITH SEASONED CREAM

This rich-tasting combination makes a superb side dish for broiled meat, fish and poultry, or serve it as a wonderful vegetarian entrée. If you use leftover rice, refresh it by placing it in a colander and pouring boiling water over it.

Makes 4 servings

¹/₂ cup + 2 tablespoons minced onions
¹/₄ cup plain nonfat yogurt
¹/₄ cup nonfat sour cream
1 small garlic clove, minced
1 teaspoon corn oil
1 small garlic clove, crushed

1 medium poblano pepper, roasted, peeled, seeded and diced (see page vi; see page ix for roasting technique)
2 cups cooked long-grain rice
3 ounces extra-sharp cheddar cheese, shredded

1. Preheat oven to 350°F. Spray 1-quart shallow baking dish with nonstick cooking spray.
2. In small bowl, combine 2 tablespoons of the onions, the yogurt, sour cream and minced garlic; set aside.
3. In medium nonstick skillet, heat oil; add remaining ¹/₂ cup onions, the crushed garlic and the pepper. Cook over medium heat, stirring frequently, 3 minutes, until vegetables are softened. Add rice, cheese and reserved yogurt mixture to onion mixture; stir to combine.
4. Transfer rice mixture to prepared baking dish; bake, covered, 30 minutes.

Each serving (1 cup) provides: ¹/₄ Fat, ¹/₂ Vegetable, 1 Protein, 1 Bread, 20 Optional Calories

Per serving: 265 Calories, 9 g Total Fat, 5 g Saturated Fat, 23 mg Cholesterol, 157 mg Sodium, 35 g Total Carbohydrate, 1 g Dietary Fiber, 11 g Protein, 221 mg Calcium

ARROZ À LA POBLANA (RICE WITH PEPPERS, CORN AND PLANTAIN)

Use this as a side dish for Turkey Molé Poblano (see page 49) or Pollo Borracho (see page 36).

Makes 4 servings

2 teaspoons corn oil
6 ounces uncooked regular (not converted) long-grain rice
¹/₂ cup minced onion
1³/₄ cups low-sodium chicken broth
1 cup fresh or frozen corn kernels (see page x for fresh corn preparation technique)
2 medium poblano peppers, roasted, peeled, seeded and thinly sliced (see page vi; see page ix for roasting technique)

¹/₂ teaspoon salt
6 ounces peeled and diced yellow-ripe plantain (¹/₂" dice) (see page vii for ingredient information)
1¹/₂ ounces *queso fresco*, soft-textured pot cheese or soaked and drained feta cheese, crumbled (see page vii for soaking information)
2 tablespoons minced fresh flat-leaf parsley

1. In medium saucepan, heat 1 teaspoon of the oil; add rice and onion. Cook over medium heat, stirring frequently, 5–7 minutes, until onion is softened and rice is lightly browned.
2. Slowly and carefully, stir broth into rice mixture. Stir in corn, peppers and salt; bring liquid to a boil. Reduce heat to low; simmer, covered, 12 minutes, until almost all of the liquid is absorbed and rice is almost tender. Remove from heat; let stand 5–10 minutes, until all of the liquid is absorbed.
3. In medium nonstick skillet, heat remaining 1 teaspoon oil; add plantain. Cook over medium heat, turning frequently, 3–5 minutes, until golden.
4. Transfer plantain to rice mixture; with fork, toss lightly to combine. Spoon rice mixture onto serving platter; sprinkle with cheese and parsley.

Each serving (1¹/₂ cups) provides: ¹/₂ Fat, ³/₄ Vegetable, ¹/₂ Protein, 2¹/₂ Breads, 10 Optional Calories

Per serving: 325 Calories, 7 g Total Fat, 3 g Saturated Fat, 8 mg Cholesterol, 412 mg Sodium, 60 g Total Carbohydrate, 2 g Dietary Fiber, 9 g Protein, 91 mg Calcium

MEXICAN POLENTA

Polenta is the perfect match for grilled fish and poultry; add a tossed salad and you have a fabulous meal.

Makes 8 servings

1 teaspoon salt
2 cups uncooked yellow cornmeal
1 medium red bell pepper, roasted, peeled, seeded and diced (see page ix for roasting technique)
1 medium poblano pepper, roasted, peeled, seeded and diced (see page vi; see page ix for roasting technique)

$^1/_2$ cup fresh or frozen corn kernels (see page x for fresh corn preparation technique)
$^1/_2$ teaspoon garlic powder
$^1/_2$ teaspoon ground cumin
$^1/_2$ teaspoon mild or hot chili powder

1. Spray 8" square glass baking dish with nonstick cooking spray.
2. In large saucepan, combine 6 cups water and the salt; bring to a boil over high heat. With wooden spoon, stir boiling water briskly, creating a whirl-pool; continuing to stir briskly, gradually add cornmeal in a steady stream, breaking up any lumps as they form. Reduce heat to low; cook, stirring occasionally, 20 minutes, until mixture thickens and pulls away from sides of saucepan.
3. Add bell and poblano peppers, corn, garlic powder, cumin and chili powder to cornmeal mixture; stir to combine. Transfer mixture to prepared baking dish; let stand 30 minutes, until firm. Cut into sixteen 2" squares.

Each serving (2 squares) provides: $^1/_2$ Vegetable, 2 Breads, 10 Optional Calories

Per serving: 143 Calories, 1 g Total Fat, 0 g Saturated Fat, 0 mg Cholesterol, 280 mg Sodium, 30 g Total Carbohydrate, 2 g Dietary Fiber, 4 g Protein, 8 mg Calcium

Swiss Chard with Potatoes

This simple, savory vegetable dish can be turned into a main course with the addition of a little cheese. It is so flavorful that it may make vegetables your favorite part of the meal!

Makes 4 servings

2 teaspoons corn oil
1 cup thinly sliced onions
1 medium jalapeño pepper, seeded, deveined and thinly sliced (see page v)
1 cup stewed tomatoes

10 ounces diced red potatoes (³/₄" dice)
¹/₂ cup vegetable broth or low-sodium chicken broth
10 cups lightly packed Swiss chard leaves, well rinsed and cut crosswise into 1" strips

1. In medium saucepan, heat oil; add onions and pepper. Cook over medium heat, stirring frequently, 10–12 minutes, until onions are golden brown.
2. Add tomatoes to onion mixture; bring to a boil over high heat. Cook, stirring constantly, 2 minutes, until mixture is slightly reduced in volume.
3. Add potatoes and broth to tomato mixture; bring liquid to a boil. Reduce heat to low; simmer, covered, 10–12 minutes, until potatoes are tender and liquid is reduced in volume to about ¹/₃ cup.
4. Add Swiss chard to potato mixture; cook 3 minutes, just until Swiss chard is wilted.

Each serving (1¹/₄ cups) provides: ¹/₂ Fat, 6¹/₄ Vegetables, ¹/₂ Bread, 5 Optional Calories

Per serving with vegetable broth: 135 Calories, 3 g Total Fat, 0 g Saturated Fat, 0 mg Cholesterol, 536 mg Sodium, 26 g Total Carbohydrate, 3 g Dietary Fiber, 5 g Protein, 91 mg Calcium

Per serving with chicken broth: 136 Calories, 3 g Total Fat, 0 g Saturated Fat, 0 mg Cholesterol, 426 mg Sodium, 25 g Total Carbohydrate, 3 g Dietary Fiber, 5 g Protein, 93 mg Calcium

POTATO-PEPPER GRATIN

This layered potato casserole is a wonderfully hearty side dish for meats and poultry. For a fiery zip, use hot chile peppers.

Makes 4 servings

15 ounces potatoes, pared and very thinly sliced
1 tablespoon all-purpose flour
1/2 cup drained canned mild or hot chopped green chile peppers
1/4 cup chopped fresh cilantro
2 tablespoons grated Parmesan cheese

1 teaspoon grated lemon zest*
2 garlic cloves, minced
1/4 teaspoon freshly ground black pepper
Pinch salt
3/4 cup skim milk

1. Preheat oven to 350°F. Spray 4-cup soufflé dish or 8" square baking pan with nonstick cooking spray.
2. Layer one third of the potatoes into prepared dish; sprinkle with half of the flour. Top potato mixture with half of the chile peppers, cilantro, cheese, zest, garlic, black pepper and salt. Repeat layers; top with remaining potatoes.
3. Pour milk evenly over potato mixture, patting down with back of wooden spoon to allow milk to penetrate layers; bake, covered, 1 hour, until potatoes are tender. Remove cover; bake 20 minutes longer, until top of gratin is lightly browned. Remove from oven; let stand 10 minutes.

Each serving provides: 1/4 Vegetable, 3/4 Bread, 40 Optional Calories

Per serving: 128 Calories, 1 g Total Fat, 1 g Saturated Fat, 3 mg Cholesterol, 359 mg Sodium, 24 g Total Carbohydrate, 2 g Dietary Fiber, 5 g Protein, 108 mg Calcium

* *The zest of the lemon is the peel without any of the pith (white membrane). To remove zest from lemon, use a zester or the side of a vegetable grater; wrap lemon in plastic wrap and refrigerate for use at another time.*

TORTILLAS, CRACKERS AND BREADS

Corn Tortillas
Flour Tortillas
Corn Crackers
Ship's Crackers
Bolillos
Mexi-Cheese Sticks
Mexican Corn Bread
Wild Rice and Jalapeño Pancakes
Conchas (Sweet Rolls with Chocolate)
Pan de Muertos
Torta de Arroz con Elote (Rice and Corn Cake)

CORN TORTILLAS

Preparing these tortillas does take some practice, so don't despair if your first efforts fall apart or are tough. If you plan to make your own tortillas regularly, a tortilla press is a good investment. Once cooled, tortillas can be served immediately or wrapped and frozen for future use.

Makes 10 servings

2 cups minus 2 tablespoons *masa harina* (corn flour)

¹/₂ teaspoon salt (optional)

1. In medium bowl or food processor, combine *masa harina* and salt if using. Add 1¹/₄ cups water; knead well or process until dough is soft and smooth, but not sticky; add more water, 1 teaspoon at a time, if needed.
2. Divide dough into 10 equal pieces. Form each piece into a ball; wrap individually in plastic wrap.
3. Heat medium nonstick griddle or heavy nonstick skillet over medium heat until a drop of water dances on surface.
4. Place 1 dough ball on 12" square of plastic wrap; cover with another square. With rolling pin or tortilla press, flatten dough into 6" circle about ¹/₈" thick. Carefully remove top sheet of plastic wrap. Sliding your hand under the bottom sheet of plastic wrap, lift tortilla; turn it onto your other hand. Carefully peel off plastic wrap; gently place tortilla on heated griddle.
5. Cook tortilla 15 seconds; turn over carefully. Cook 30 seconds longer, until underside of tortilla is opaque and spotted with brown. Turn over again; cook 15 seconds longer, until firm and slightly puffed. Transfer cooked tortilla to tea towel–lined serving bowl or basket.
6. Repeat with remaining dough balls, making 9 more tortillas.

Each serving (1 tortilla) provides: 1 Bread

Per serving with salt: 78 Calories, 0 g Total Fat, 0 g Saturated Fat, 0 mg Cholesterol, 110 mg Sodium, 17 g Total Carbohydrate, 0 g Dietary Fiber, 2 g Protein, 31 mg Calcium

Per serving without salt: 78 Calories, 0 g Total Fat, 0 g Saturated Fat, 0 mg Cholesterol, 1 mg Sodium, 16 g Total Carbohydrate, 0 g Dietary Fiber, 2 g Protein, 30 mg Calcium

FLOUR TORTILLAS

This dough is easier to handle than the dough for corn tortillas, so you might want to try this recipe before preparing corn tortillas. The tortillas freeze well, so prepare enough to have on hand as you need them.

Makes 12 servings

2$^1/_4$ cups all-purpose flour $^3/_4$ teaspoon salt
2 tablespoons corn oil

1. In a small freezer-safe bowl, combine $^1/_3$ cup of the flour and the oil, stirring well. Freeze, covered, 1 hour.
2. Spray medium bowl with nonstick cooking spray.
3. In separate medium bowl or food processor, combine all but 1 tablespoon of the remaining flour and the salt; with on-off motion, pulse processor until mixture is blended. Add reserved flour-oil mixture and $^1/_2$ cup water; knead well or process until dough is soft and smooth, but not sticky; add more water, 1 teaspoon at a time, if needed.
4. Divide dough into 12 equal pieces. Form each piece into a ball; place in prepared bowl. Let stand, covered, 30 minutes.
5. Heat medium nonstick griddle or heavy nonstick skillet over medium heat until a drop of water dances on surface.
6. Sprinkle work surface with remaining 1 tablespoon flour; transfer 1 dough ball to prepared surface. With rolling pin, flatten dough into 6" circle about $^1/_8$" thick. Carefully transfer tortilla to heated griddle.
7. Cook tortilla 5 seconds; turn over carefully. Cook 5 seconds longer, until underside of tortilla is opaque and spotted with brown, and tortilla is slightly puffed. Transfer cooked tortilla to tea towel–lined serving bowl or basket.
8. Repeat with remaining dough balls, making 11 more tortillas.

Each serving (1 tortilla) provides: $^1/_2$ Fat, 1 Bread

Per serving: 106 Calories, 3 g Total Fat, 0 g Saturated Fat, 0 mg Cholesterol, 138 mg Sodium, 18 g Total Carbohydrate, 1 g Dietary Fiber, 2 g Protein, 4 mg Calcium

CORN CRACKERS

These very crisp, thin crackers have a delicious corn taste that goes well with soups and cheeses, but they are also great on their own.

Makes 4 servings

³/₄ cup *masa harina*
  (corn flour)
3 tablespoons all-purpose flour
2 teaspoons granulated sugar
1 teaspoon double-acting
  baking powder

³/₄ teaspoon salt
1 cup skim milk
1 egg, beaten
1 tablespoon corn oil
1 tablespoon stick margarine,
  melted

1. Preheat oven to 350°F. Spray baking sheet with nonstick cooking spray.
2. In medium bowl, combine *masa harina*, flour, sugar, baking powder and salt. Add milk, egg, oil, and margarine; with wire whisk, blend until smooth.
3. Drop batter by teaspoonful, 2" apart, onto prepared baking sheet, making 24 crackers; bake 7–10 minutes, until golden brown on bottom. Turn crackers over; bake 6–8 minutes longer, until golden brown around edges. Turn oven off; let crackers stand in oven 15 minutes. Transfer crackers to wire rack to cool.

Each serving (6 crackers) provides: ¹/₄ Milk, ¹/₂ Fats, ¹/₄ Protein, 1¹/₄ Breads, 10 Optional Calories

Per serving: 205 Calories, 9 g Total Fat, 1 g Saturated Fat, 54 mg Cholesterol, 616 mg Sodium, 26 g Total Carbohydrate, 0 g Dietary Fiber, 6 g Protein, 184 mg Calcium

VARIATION:

Buttery Corn Crackers: Substitute 1 tablespoon lightly salted butter, melted, for the margarine; reduce Fat Selection to ³/₄ and increase Optional Calories to 35.

Per serving: 205 Calories, 9 g Total Fat, 3 g Saturated Fat, 62 mg Cholesterol, 612 mg Sodium, 26 g Total Carbohydrate, 0 g Dietary Fiber, 6 g Protein, 184 mg Calcium

SHIP'S CRACKERS

These crunchy, puffed crackers are irresistible; serve them with soup or salads, or with steaming cups of Mexican Hot Chocolate (see page 194). They will keep for weeks in an airtight container.

Makes 16 servings

1 cup + 3 tablespoons lukewarm (110°F) water

2 tablespoons unsalted stick margarine, at room temperature

1 envelope active dry yeast

$1^3/_4$ teaspoons salt

$^1/_2$ teaspoon granulated sugar

$3^1/_4$ cups + 2 tablespoons all-purpose flour

1. Spray 2 shiny baking sheets with nonstick cooking spray.
2. In medium bowl, combine lukewarm water, margarine, yeast, salt and sugar; let stand 10 minutes, until margarine is almost melted.
3. In large bowl or food processor, combine flour and water mixture; knead 10 minutes or process 1 minute, until dough is smooth and elastic.
4. Transfer dough to work surface. Divide dough into 32 equal pieces; roll each piece into a ball. Place balls 2" apart on prepared baking sheets; spray balls lightly with nonstick cooking spray. Let balls rise in warm, draft-free place, covered loosely with plastic wrap, $1-1^1/_2$ hours, until almost doubled in size.
5. With fingertips, press each ball to $^1/_4$" thickness; let rise in warm, draft-free place, covered loosely with plastic wrap, 1 hour, until soft and puffy.
6. Preheat oven to 300°F. Adjust oven racks to divide oven into thirds.
7. Place one baking sheet on each oven rack; bake 45 minutes. Switch and rotate baking sheets; bake 45 minutes longer, until crackers are lightly browned and crisp. Transfer crackers to wire rack to cool.

Each serving (2 crackers) provides: $^1/_4$ Fat, 1 Bread, 15 Optional Calories

Per serving: 112 Calories, 2 g Total Fat, 0 g Saturated Fat, 0 mg Cholesterol, 241 mg Sodium, 20 g Total Carbohydrate, 1 g Dietary Fiber, 3 g Protein, 6 mg Calcium

BOLILLOS

These crusty rolls surprise visitors to Mexico, who expect tortillas to be the only type of bread served. They are simple to make and wonderful for sandwiches.

Makes 12 servings

1 envelope active dry yeast	3$^{1}/_{4}$ cups all-purpose flour
1$^{1}/_{4}$ cups lukewarm (110°F) water	$^{1}/_{4}$ cup whole-wheat flour
	1$^{1}/_{2}$ teaspoons salt

1. Spray large bowl with nonstick cooking spray.
2. In small bowl, sprinkle yeast over lukewarm water; stir to combine. Let stand 10 minutes, until yeast is dissolved.
3. In large bowl or food processor, combine all but 2 tablespoons of the all-purpose flour, and the whole-wheat flour and salt; with on-off motion, pulse processor until mixture is blended. With machine on, add yeast mixture; stir until well blended or process 1 minute, until dough forms a ball and cleans sides of bowl.
4. Sprinkle work surface with 1 tablespoon of the remaining flour; transfer dough to prepared surface. Knead dough 10 minutes, until smooth and elastic.
5. Transfer dough to prepared bowl; let rise in warm, draft-free place, covered, 1 hour, until doubled in size.
6. Punch down dough. Sprinkle work surface with remaining 1 tablespoon flour; transfer dough to prepared surface. Divide dough into 12 equal pieces; form each piece into an oval with pointed ends.
7. Spray a shiny baking sheet with nonstick cooking spray; place ovals 3" apart on prepared baking sheet. Let rolls rise in warm, draft-free place, covered loosely with plastic wrap, 1 hour, until doubled in size.
8. Preheat oven to 400°F. Adjust oven rack to divide oven in half.
9. With sharp knife, make a shallow slit in top of each oval, beginning and ending $^{1}/_{2}$" from pointed ends. Bake in center of oven 20–25 minutes, until rolls are golden brown and sound hollow when tapped. Transfer rolls to wire rack to cool.

Each serving (1 roll) provides: 1$^{1}/_{2}$ Breads, 5 Optional Calories

Per serving: 135 Calories, 1 g Total Fat, 0 g Saturated Fat, 0 mg Cholesterol, 276 mg Sodium, 28 g Total Carbohydrate, 1 g Dietary Fiber, 4 g Protein, 8 mg Calcium

MEXI-CHEESE STICKS

These sticks are a great party treat that can be prepared in advance because they freeze beautifully. Just reheat them in a 375°F oven about 4–5 minutes before serving.

Makes 8 servings

1 tablespoon all-purpose flour
10 ounces ready-made pizza dough (unbaked)
1 teaspoon mild or hot chili powder
1/2 teaspoon garlic powder

1 medium jalapeño pepper, seeded, deveined and minced (see page v)
1 1/2 ounces grated Parmesan cheese
1 1/2 ounces sharp cheddar cheese, finely shredded

1. Preheat oven to 400°F. Spray baking sheet with nonstick cooking spray.
2. Sprinkle work surface with flour; with rolling pin, roll out dough on prepared surface to form 18 × 11" rectangle. Beginning at short end, sprinkle half of dough with chili and garlic powders.
3. In small bowl, combine pepper and Parmesan and cheddar cheeses; sprinkle over seasoned half of dough.
4. Fold unseasoned half of dough over seasoned half, forming 9 × 11" rectangle; press edges together to seal. With rolling pin, roll dough several times to press filling into dough.
5. Cut dough in half, forming two 4 1/2 × 11" rectangles; cut into forty-eight 4 1/2" strips. Twist each strip 6 or 7 times; place on prepared baking sheet, pressing ends into pan to hold in place (if any filling escaped while twisting, sprinkle over dough). Bake 15 minutes, until golden brown.

Each serving (6 sticks) provides: 1/4 Vegetable, 1/2 Protein, 1 1/4 Breads, 5 Optional Calories

Per serving: 147 Calories, 5 g Total Fat, 2 g Saturated Fat, 10 mg Cholesterol, 330 mg Sodium, 18 g Total Carbohydrate, 1 g Dietary Fiber, 7 g Protein, 113 mg Calcium

MEXICAN CORN BREAD

Mexican cuisine uses corn in myriad ways; here it's featured in a classic corn bread.

Makes 6 servings

2 tablespoons vegetable oil
2 medium jalapeño peppers, seeded, deveined and finely chopped (see page v)
$^1/_2$ cup chopped onion
$^1/_2$ cup diced red bell pepper
1 cup minus 1 tablespoon all-purpose flour
1 cup uncooked yellow cornmeal
1 tablespoon double-acting baking powder

1 teaspoon salt
1 teaspoon granulated sugar
1 cup drained cooked fresh or frozen corn kernels (see page x for fresh corn preparation technique)
$^1/_2$ cup low-fat (1%) milk
$^1/_2$ cup plain nonfat yogurt
1 egg white

1. Preheat oven to 400°F. Spray 8" square baking pan with nonstick cooking spray.
2. In large nonstick skillet, heat oil; add jalapeño peppers, onion and bell pepper. Cook over medium heat, stirring frequently, 8 minutes, until vegetables are tender. Transfer to small bowl; cool to room temperature.
3. Meanwhile, in medium bowl, combine flour, cornmeal, baking powder, salt and sugar.
4. Add corn, milk, yogurt and egg white to onion mixture; stir to combine. Add corn mixture to flour mixture; stir just until combined (do not overmix). Transfer mixture to prepared baking pan; bake 30 minutes, until corn bread pulls away from sides of pan. Transfer pan to wire rack to cool.

Each serving provides: 1 Fat, $^3/_4$ Vegetable, $2^1/_2$ Breads, 25 Optional Calories

Per serving: 261 Calories, 6 g Total Fat, 1 g Saturated Fat, 1 mg Cholesterol, 651 mg Sodium, 46 g Total Carbohydrate, 3 g Dietary Fiber, 7 g Protein, 209 mg Calcium

WILD RICE AND JALAPEÑO PANCAKES

These different pancakes are an exciting accompaniment to grilled fish and chicken.

Makes 8 servings

1 cup + 2 tablespoons all-purpose flour

$^1/_2$ cup + 1 tablespoon *masa harina* (corn flour; see page viii)

$^1/_2$ teaspoon double-acting baking powder

$^1/_2$ teaspoon salt

$^1/_4$ teaspoon mild or hot chili powder

$1^1/_2$ cups evaporated skimmed milk

$^1/_2$ cup egg substitute

1 tablespoon + 1 teaspoon canola oil

1 cup cooked wild rice

1 medium jalapeño pepper, seeded, deveined and finely chopped (see page v)

3 tablespoons finely chopped scallions (white portion with some green)

$^1/_3$ cup diced tomato

Finely chopped fresh cilantro, to garnish

1. In large bowl, combine flour, *masa harina*, baking powder, salt and chili powder. In medium bowl, with wire whisk, combine milk, egg substitute and oil. Add wet ingredients to dry; stir until combined and smooth. Add rice, pepper and scallions; stir to combine.*
2. Spray large nonstick skillet with nonstick cooking spray; place over medium heat. Pour batter by 2 tablespoonsful into skillet, making four 3" pancakes. Cook 3–4 minutes, until pancakes are browned on bottom; turn and cook 2 minutes longer, until other side is browned. With spatula, transfer pancakes to plate; keep warm. Repeat with remaining batter, making 28 more pancakes. Serve pancakes topped with tomato and garnished with cilantro.

Each serving (4 pancakes + 2 teaspoons tomato) provides: $^1/_4$ Milk, $^1/_2$ Fat, $^1/_4$ Vegetable, $^1/_4$ Protein, $1^1/_4$ Breads, 20 Optional Calories

Per serving: 190 Calories, 4 g Total Fat, 0 g Saturated Fat, 2 mg Cholesterol, 250 mg Sodium, 30 g Total Carbohydrate, 1 g Dietary Fiber, 9 g Protein, 179 mg Calcium

* Recipe may be prepared ahead up to this point; refrigerate covered, up to 2 hours.

CONCHAS (SWEET ROLLS WITH CHOCOLATE)

The name *concha,* which means "shell," was given to these light, chocolate-topped rolls because of the shell pattern stamped into the icing. They go well with Café de Olla (see page 195) for an afternoon coffee hour.

Makes 12 servings

Sweet Rolls:

1¼ teaspoons active dry yeast

3 tablespoons lukewarm (110°F) water

2½ cups all-purpose flour

¼ cup granulated sugar

¼ teaspoon salt

¾ cup egg substitute

1 tablespoon corn oil

Icing:

¼ cup confectioners sugar

1 tablespoon unsweetened cocoa powder

½ teaspoon ground cinnamon

2 tablespoons skim milk

1. Spray large bowl with nonstick cooking spray.

2. In small bowl, sprinkle yeast over lukewarm water; stir to combine. Let stand 10 minutes, until yeast is dissolved.

3. In food processor, combine all but 1 tablespoon of the flour, and the sugar and salt; with on-off motion, pulse processor until mixture is blended. Add egg substitute and oil to flour mixture; process to combine. With machine on, add yeast mixture; process 1 minute, until dough forms a ball and cleans sides of bowl.

4. Transfer dough to prepared bowl; press down. Refrigerate dough, covered loosely with plastic wrap, 8–12 hours.

5. Punch down dough. Sprinkle work surface with remaining 1 tablespoon flour; transfer dough to prepared surface. Divide dough into 12 equal pieces; form each piece into a ball.

6. Spray shiny baking sheet with nonstick cooking spray. Place balls 2" apart on prepared baking sheet; spray balls lightly with nonstick cooking spray. Let balls rise in warm, draft-free place, covered loosely with plastic wrap, 1 hour, until almost doubled in size.

7. Preheat oven to 350°F. Adjust oven racks to divide oven into thirds.

8. Bake in upper third of oven 20–25 minutes, until rolls are lightly browned around edges and sound hollow when tapped. Transfer rolls to wire rack to cool slightly.

9. Meanwhile, to prepare icing, in small bowl, combine sugar, cocoa and cinnamon. Add milk; stir until mixture is smooth enough to spread.

10. Spread an equal amount of icing on each warm roll; cool. With round cookie cutter or sharp knife, make concentric semicircles into icing, forming a shell pattern.

Each serving (1 sweet roll) provides: ¹/₄ Fat, ¹/₄ Protein, 1 Bread, 40 Optional Calories

Per serving: 143 Calories, 2 g Total Fat, 0 g Saturated Fat, 0 mg Cholesterol, 72 mg Sodium, 27 g Total Carbohydrate, 1 g Dietary Fiber, 5 g Protein, 14 mg Calcium

PAN DE MUERTOS

A tradition for All Souls' Day, celebrated every November 2 to commemorate the release of souls from purgatory, this bread is a much lightened version of the usual, which is laden with egg yolks, lard and butter. Children will enjoy forming "bones" out of the dough to decorate the loaf.

Makes 8 servings

1 envelope active dry yeast
¹/₂ cup lukewarm (110°F) water
2 cups minus 2 tablespoons
 all-purpose flour
¹/₄ cup + 1 tablespoon
 granulated sugar
³/₄ teaspoon salt

¹/₄ cup egg substitute
2 teaspoons corn oil
1 teaspoon grated orange zest*
4 drops yellow food coloring
2 teaspoons unsalted stick
 margarine, melted

1. In small bowl, sprinkle yeast over lukewarm water; stir to combine. Let stand 10 minutes, until yeast is dissolved.
2. In large bowl or food processor, combine all but 1 tablespoon of the flour, all but 1 teaspoon of the sugar and the salt; with on-off motion, pulse processor until mixture is blended.
3. Add egg substitute, oil, zest and food coloring to yeast mixture; stir to combine. If using large bowl, stir egg mixture into flour mixture, beating vigorously to combine. Transfer mixture to work surface; knead 10 minutes, until dough is soft, springy and elastic. If using food processor, with machine on, slowly add yeast mixture to flour mixture; process 1 minute, until dough forms a ball and cleans sides of bowl.
4. Spray clean large bowl with nonstick cooking spray; transfer dough to prepared bowl. Let rise in warm, draft-free place, loosely covered, 1 hour, until doubled in size.
5. Spray 8" springform or round cake pan with nonstick cooking spray.
6. Punch down dough. Sprinkle work surface with remaining 1 tablespoon flour; transfer dough to prepared surface. Cut off one quarter of the dough; set aside. Form remaining dough into ball; press gently into prepared pan.
7. With thumb, make deep indentations into center of dough, forming a pattern that looks like 2 eyes, a nose and a mouth. Shape reserved dough into 4 bone-shaped pieces; place 2 "bones," crisscrossed, above "eyes" and 2 "bones," crisscrossed, below "mouth." Let dough rise, covered loosely with plastic wrap, 1 hour, until doubled in size.†

8. Adjust oven rack to divide oven in half.

9. Place dough in center of cold oven; set oven temperature to 350°F. Bake 20 minutes.

10. Spray foil-lined baking sheet with nonstick cooking spray. Carefully remove bread from pan and place on prepared baking sheet; leave oven on. Brush top of bread evenly with margarine; sprinkle with reserved 1 teaspoon sugar. Bake 10 minutes longer, until bread sounds hollow when tapped. Transfer bread to wire rack to cool; slice.

Each serving ($^1/_8$ of bread) provides: $^1/_2$ Fat, $1^1/_4$ Breads, 35 Optional Calories

Per serving: 165 Calories, 3 g Total Fat, 0 g Saturated Fat, 0 mg Cholesterol, 220 mg Sodium, 31 g Total Carbohydrate, 1 g Dietary Fiber, 4 g Protein, 9 mg Calcium

    * *The zest of the orange is the peel without any of the pith (white membrane). To remove zest from orange, use a zester or the side of a vegetable grater; wrap orange in plastic wrap and refrigerate for use at another time.*

    †*Pattern becomes blurred as dough rises and bakes. If desired, for a clearer pattern, place "bones" separately on baking sheet; bake just until golden brown. Before brushing bread with margarine, spread bottom of "bones" with $^1/_2$ egg white; place on bread. Continue as directed.*

Per serving with egg white: 166 Calories, 3 g Total Fat, 0 g Saturated Fat, 0 mg Cholesterol, 223 mg Sodium, 31 g Total Carbohydrate, 1 g Dietary Fiber, 4 g Protein, 10 mg Calcium

VARIATION:

Butter-Topped Pan de Muertos: Substitute 2 teaspoons sweet butter, melted, for the margarine; reduce Fat Selection to $^1/_4$ and increase Optional Calories to 45.

Per serving: 165 Calories, 3 g Total Fat, 1 g Saturated Fat, 3 mg Cholesterol, 220 mg Sodium, 31 g Total Carbohydrate, 1 g Dietary Fiber, 4 g Protein, 10 mg Calcium

TORTA DE ARROZ CON ELOTE (RICE AND CORN CAKE)

Serve this unusual quick bread as a side dish for a brunch or light supper. It's lovely for mid-afternoon with Mexican Hot Chocolate (see page 194).

Makes 8 servings

³/₄ cup rice flour*

2 teaspoons granulated sugar

1¹/₂ teaspoons double-acting baking powder

¹/₂ teaspoon salt

1 medium poblano pepper, roasted, peeled, seeded and diced (see page vi; see page ix for roasting technique)

3 ounces extra-sharp cheddar cheese, shredded

1 tablespoon grated Parmesan cheese

¹/₂ cup fresh or frozen corn kernels (see page x for fresh corn preparation technique)

¹/₂ cup egg substitute

2 tablespoons skim milk

1 tablespoon + 1 teaspoon corn oil

2 egg whites, at room temperature

1. Preheat oven to 350°F. Adjust oven racks to divide oven into thirds. Spray 8" springform or round cake pan with nonstick cooking spray.
2. In large bowl, combine flour, sugar, baking powder and salt. Add pepper and cheddar and Parmesan cheeses; toss to combine. Set aside.
3. In food processor or blender, combine corn, egg substitute, milk and oil; with on-off motion, pulse processor until mixture is coarsely ground. Add corn mixture to flour mixture; stir just until combined.
4. In medium bowl, with electric mixer on high speed, beat egg whites until stiff but not dry; fold into corn mixture. Transfer mixture to prepared pan; bake 30–35 minutes, until toothpick inserted in center comes out clean. Transfer pan to wire rack; cool 10 minutes. Remove cake from pan; serve warm or at room temperature.

Each serving (¹/₈ of cake) provides: ¹/₂ Fat, ¹/₄ Vegetable, ³/₄ Protein, ¹/₂ Bread, 25 Optional Calories

Per serving: 150 Calories, 6 g Total Fat, 3 g Saturated Fat, 12 mg Cholesterol, 348 mg Sodium, 16 g Total Carbohydrate, 1 g Dietary Fiber, 7 g Protein, 150 mg Calcium

* Rice flour is available in health food stores and some Asian groceries.

9

SAUCES, SALSAS
AND RELISHES

Molé Poblano
Ranchero Sauce
Tequila Hot Sauce
Cooked Red Sauce
Cooked Green Sauce
Sweet and Hot Pepper Purée
Salsa Cruda
Salsa Verde
Salsa Chipotle
Salsa X-Ni-Pek
Tomato-Melon Salsa with Tortilla Chips
Chiles en Escabeche (Pickled Peppers)
Pickled Onions

Molé Poblano

This version of an ancient and exquisite sauce has a fraction of the original's fat. It *is* a bit time consuming to make, but it is well worth it. Since the recipe makes a quart of rich, dark sauce, divide it into 1-cup portions and freeze them so you'll have them on hand to use in recipes such as Turkey Molé Poblano (see page 49). The sauce is also delicious with chicken, pork, Cornish hens and beef.

Makes 16 servings

Two 6" corn tortillas, torn into bite-size pieces
1 cup stewed tomatoes
1 tablespoon unsweetened cocoa powder
1 teaspoon pureed canned chipotle peppers in adobo sauce (see page vi for ingredient information)
1/2 teaspoon ground aniseed
1/4 teaspoon freshly ground black pepper
1/4 teaspoon ground cinnamon
Pinch ground cloves
1 ounce blanched almonds
1 tablespoon sesame seeds
1/4 teaspoon coriander seeds
1 tablespoon + 1 teaspoon corn oil
8 medium dried mulato peppers, seeded and torn into pieces (see page ix for preparation technique)

3 medium dried pasilla peppers, seeded and torn into pieces (see page ix for preparation technique)
2 medium dried ancho peppers, seeded and torn into pieces (see page ix for preparation technique)
Boiling water
1 cup sliced onions
1/2 cup raisins
1 garlic clove, crushed
1 cup low-sodium chicken broth
1 tablespoon + 1 teaspoon granulated sugar
1/2 teaspoon salt

1. Preheat oven to 325°F. Spray baking sheet with nonstick cooking spray.
2. Place tortilla pieces in a single layer on baking sheet; bake 20–30 minutes, until golden and crisp.
3. Meanwhile, in large bowl, combine tomatoes, cocoa, pureed peppers, aniseed, black pepper, cinnamon and cloves. Add baked tortilla pieces; stir to combine.

4. In medium nonstick skillet, toast almonds, sesame seeds and coriander seeds over low heat, stirring constantly, 5–7 minutes, until almonds are golden brown; stir into tomato mixture.
5. In same skillet, heat 2 teaspoons of the oil; add mulato, pasilla and ancho peppers. Cook over medium heat, stirring frequently, 2 minutes, until peppers are browned. With slotted spoon, transfer peppers to medium bowl; add boiling water to cover. Let stand 1 hour.
6. Meanwhile, in same skillet, heat remaining 2 teaspoons oil; add onions. Cook over medium heat, stirring frequently, 10–12 minutes, until onions are golden brown. Add raisins and garlic; cook, stirring frequently, 2 minutes longer. Add to tomato mixture.
7. Drain peppers; add to tomato mixture.
8. In batches, transfer tomato mixture to food processor or blender; purée until smooth, adding broth as needed.
9. Place medium sieve over same large bowl. Strain tomato mixture through sieve, pressing with back of wooden spoon; discard solids. Stir remaining broth, the sugar and salt into tomato mixture; refrigerate, covered, until thickened and chilled.

Each serving (¹/₄ cup) provides: ¹/₄ Fat, ¹/₄ Fruit, 1 Vegetable, 30 Optional Calories

Per serving: 97 Calories, 5 g Total Fat, 1 g Saturated Fat, 0 mg Cholesterol, 131 mg Sodium, 15 g Total Carbohydrate, 1 g Dietary Fiber, 3 g Protein, 46 mg Calcium

RANCHERO SAUCE

This is not the standard ranchero sauce, which uses fresh chile peppers; the dried ones here give it a rich, almost smoky flavor that complements light omelets, chicken and pork.

Makes 4 servings

1 teaspoon corn oil	1¹/₂ cups stewed tomatoes
1 medium dried mulato or ancho pepper, seeded and torn into pieces (see page ix for preparation technique)	1 medium jalapeño pepper, seeded and deveined (see page v)
Boiling water	2 garlic cloves, peeled
	2 tablespoons chopped onion

1. In small nonstick skillet, heat oil; add mulato pepper. Cook over medium heat, stirring constantly, 30 seconds, until softened. Transfer cooked pepper to small bowl; add boiling water to cover. Let stand 15 minutes; drain.
2. Transfer cooked pepper to food processor or blender. Add ³/₄ cup of the tomatoes; purée until smooth. Add remaining ³/₄ cup tomatoes, and the jalapeño pepper and garlic; process until coarsely pureed.
3. In same skillet, cook onion over medium heat, stirring frequently, 8–10 minutes, until lightly browned.
4. Add pepper mixture to cooked onion; cook over high heat, stirring frequently, 3–4 minutes, until heated.

Each serving (¹/₃ cup) provides: 1¹/₄ Vegetables, 10 Optional Calories

Per serving: 52 Calories, 2 g Total Fat, 0 g Saturated Fat, 0 mg Cholesterol, 245 mg Sodium, 9 g Total Carbohydrate, 2 g Dietary Fiber, 2 g Protein, 41 mg Calcium

154 lbs

XMAS
95

TEQUILA HOT SAUCE

This is a nice change from other hot sauces. Refrigerate at least 2 days before using; it will keep indefinitely. Use it in soups, sauces, stews and salad dressing, or add a teaspoon or two to gingerbread or spice cake batter for an elusive touch of heat.

Makes 60 servings

20 medium dried chiles de arbol, seeded (see page ix for preparation technique)

4 medium dried guajillo peppers, seeded (see page ix for preparation technique)

1 tablespoon sesame seeds

$^1/_4$ teaspoon cumin seeds

2 tablespoons shelled raw pumpkin seeds

2 large garlic cloves, unpeeled

1 teaspoon dried oregano leaves

1 teaspoon salt

4 whole allspice

2 whole cloves

$^3/_4$ cup cider vinegar

1 fluid ounce (2 tablespoons) tequila

1. Place chiles de arbol and guajillo peppers in blender; set aside.
2. In small skillet, cook sesame and cumin seeds over medium-low heat, stirring constantly, 3–5 minutes, until sesame seeds are golden brown; transfer to blender with peppers.
3. In same skillet, cook pumpkin seeds over medium-low heat, stirring constantly, 3–5 minutes, until popped and golden brown; transfer to blender with peppers.
4. In same skillet, toast garlic over medium heat, stirring frequently, until charred on all sides. Remove from skillet; let cool. Peel garlic; add to blender with peppers.
5. Add oregano, salt, allspice and cloves to peppers; process until finely ground. With machine on, slowly add enough vinegar to form a smooth purée. Add remaining vinegar and tequila; purée until smooth.
6. Place medium sieve over small bowl. Strain pepper mixture through sieve, pressing with back of wooden spoon; discard solids. Add enough water to make $1^1/_4$ cups sauce; refrigerate, covered, at least 2 days.

Each serving (1 teaspoon) provides: $^1/_2$ Vegetable; 5 Optional Calories

Per serving: 21 Calories, 1 g Total Fat, 0 g Saturated Fat, 0 mg Cholesterol, 38 mg Sodium, 4 g Total Carbohydrate, 0 g Dietary Fiber, 0 g Protein, 11 mg Calcium

COOKED RED SAUCE

Use this thick, savory sauce for Chilequiles (see page 114) or to top enchiladas, tacos and tamales. Once prepared, it will keep in the refrigerator for up to 3 days.

Makes 4 servings

1 teaspoon corn oil
$^1/_4$ cup chopped onion
1 medium jalapeño pepper, seeded, deveined and chopped (see page v)
12 large plum tomatoes, halved and roasted (see page viii for roasting technique)
2 large garlic cloves, roasted and peeled (see page viii for roasting technique)

$^1/_2$ cup vegetable broth or low-sodium chicken broth
1 teaspoon pureed canned chipotle peppers in adobo sauce (see page vi for ingredient information)
Pinch salt

1. In medium skillet, heat oil; add onion and jalapeño pepper. Cook over medium heat, stirring frequently, 8–10 minutes, until onion is lightly browned.
2. Transfer onion mixture to food processor or blender. Add tomatoes and garlic; purée until smooth.
3. Return tomato mixture to same skillet; cook over high heat, stirring frequently, 5 minutes, until very thick. Add broth, chipotle peppers and salt; stir to combine.

Each serving ($^1/_3$ cup) provides: $^1/_4$ Fat, $3^1/_2$ Vegetables, 5 Optional Calories

Per serving with vegetable broth: 56 Calories, 2 g Total Fat, 0 g Saturated Fat, 0 mg Cholesterol, 191 mg Sodium, 10 g Total Carbohydrate, 2 g Dietary Fiber, 2 g Protein, 15 mg Calcium

Per serving with chicken broth: 56 Calories, 2 g Total Fat, 0 g Saturated Fat, 0 mg Cholesterol, 81 mg Sodium, 10 g Total Carbohydrate, 2 g Dietary Fiber, 2 g Protein, 17 mg Calcium

COOKED GREEN SAUCE

This mild, garlicky green sauce is great for Chilequiles (see page 114) and is especially good with chicken and poached fish. Once prepared, it will keep in the refrigerator for up to 3 days.

Makes 4 servings

1 medium dried pasilla pepper or other dried chile pepper, seeded and torn into pieces (see page ix for preparation technique)
Boiling water
12 medium tomatillos, husked and roasted (see page viii for roasting technique)
4 large garlic cloves, roasted and peeled (see page viii for roasting technique)

1 teaspoon corn oil
$^1/_2$ cup vegetable broth or low-sodium chicken broth
1 teaspoon pureed canned chipotle peppers in adobo sauce (see page vi for ingredient information)
Pinch salt

1. In medium nonstick skillet, toast pasilla pepper or other dried chile pepper over medium heat, stirring constantly, 30 seconds, until fragrant. Transfer toasted pepper to small bowl; add boiling water to cover. Let stand 15 minutes; drain.
2. Transfer pepper to food processor or blender. Add tomatillos and garlic; purée until smooth.
3. In same skillet, heat oil; add pepper mixture. Cook over high heat, stirring frequently, 5 minutes, until very thick. Add broth, chipotle peppers and salt; stir to combine.

Each serving ($^1/_3$ cup) provides: $^1/_4$ Fat, $1^3/_4$ Vegetables, 5 Optional Calories

Per serving with vegetable broth: 96 Calories, 3 g Total Fat, 0 g Saturated Fat, 0 mg Cholesterol, 178 mg Sodium, 15 g Total Carbohydrate, 0 g Dietary Fiber, 4 g Protein, 34 mg Calcium

Per serving with chicken broth: 97 Calories, 3 g Total Fat, 0 g Saturated Fat, 0 mg Cholesterol, 67 mg Sodium, 15 g Total Carbohydrate, 0 g Dietary Fiber, 5 g Protein, 36 mg Calcium

SWEET AND HOT PEPPER PURÉE

Makes 20 servings

2 teaspoons olive oil
¹/2 cup chopped onion
6 medium red bell peppers,
  roasted, peeled, seeded and
  coarsely chopped (see page ix
  for roasting technique)

4 medium fresh hot chile peppers,
  roasted, peeled, seeded and
  coarsely chopped
  (see page v; see page xi
  for roasting technique)
Pinch salt

1. In small skillet, heat oil; add onion. Cook over medium heat, stirring frequently, 15 minutes, until deep golden brown.
2. Transfer onion to food processor. Add bell peppers, chile peppers and salt; purée until smooth.

Each serving (2 tablespoons) provides: 1 Vegetable, 5 Optional Calories

Per serving: 18 Calories, 1 g Total Fat, 0 g Saturated Fat, 0 mg Cholesterol, 8 mg Sodium, 3 g Total Carbohydrate, 1 g Dietary Fiber, 1 g Protein, 6 mg Calcium

SALSA CRUDA

Makes 8 servings

4 medium tomatoes, finely diced
¹/2 cup minced onion
1 medium jalapeño pepper,
  seeded, deveined and minced
  (see page v)

2 tablespoons minced fresh
  cilantro
1 tablespoon red wine vinegar
¹/4 teaspoon dried oregano leaves
¹/4 teaspoon salt

In medium nonreactive bowl,* combine tomatoes, onion, pepper, cilantro, vinegar, oregano and salt; let stand 30 minutes.

Each serving (¹/2 cup) provides: 1¹/4 Vegetables

Per serving: 21 Calories, 0 g Total Fat, 0 g Saturated Fat, 0 mg Cholesterol, 76 mg Sodium, 5 g Total Carbohydrate, 1 g Dietary Fiber, 1 g Protein, 8 mg Calcium

---

* It's best to marinate in bowls made of nonreactive material, such as glass, stainless steel or ceramic; ingredients such as vinegar may react with other materials, causing color and flavor changes in foods.

Salsa Verde

This sauce must be made the day you serve it; if made ahead, it loses flavor and texture. It is a fine accompaniment to fajitas, enchiladas, fish and poultry.

Makes 8 servings

6 medium tomatillos, husked and roasted (see page viii for roasting technique)
1 medium jalapeño pepper, seeded and deveined (see page v)
$^1/_4$ cup sliced scallions (white portion with some green)

6 fresh flat-leaf parsley sprigs
6 fresh cilantro sprigs
1 teaspoon fresh lime juice or white-wine vinegar
$^1/_4$ teaspoon salt

In food processor or blender, combine tomatillos, pepper, scallions, parsley, cilantro, juice and salt; purée until smooth, adding water, a teaspoon at a time, until mixture is the consistency of thin cream. Transfer to serving bowl; let stand 30 minutes, until flavors are blended.

Each serving (3 tablespoons) provides: $^1/_2$ Vegetable

Per serving with lime juice: 18 Calories, 0 g Total Fat, 0 g Saturated Fat, 0 mg Cholesterol, 69 mg Sodium, 3 g Total Carbohydrate, 0 g Dietary Fiber, 1 g Protein, 10 mg Calcium

Per serving with vinegar: 18 Calories, 0 g Total Fat, 0 g Saturated Fat, 0 mg Cholesterol, 67 mg Sodium, 3 g Total Carbohydrate, 0 g Dietary Fiber, 1 g Protein, 10 mg Calcium

SALSA CHIPOTLE

Chipotle peppers are smoked, dried jalapeño peppers, so flavorful that they give an almost meaty taste to sauces and stews. Use this sauce on meat, poultry, eggs and bean dishes, or drizzle onto tacos or over burritos. Try it on a baked potato with a dollop of plain nonfat yogurt and a sprinkling of chives. Recipe may be prepared ahead; refrigerate, covered, for up to one week. Reheat before serving.

Makes 4 servings

4 large plum tomatoes, halved and roasted (see page viii for roasting technique)

4 medium tomatillos, husked and roasted (see page viii for roasting technique)

2 large garlic cloves, roasted and peeled (see page viii for roasting technique)

1 teaspoon pureed canned chipotle peppers in adobo sauce (see page vi for ingredient information)

1 teaspoon corn oil

1. In food processor or blender, combine tomatoes, tomatillos and garlic; purée until smooth. Add peppers; process just until combined.
2. In small nonstick skillet, heat oil; add tomato mixture. Cook over high heat, stirring constantly, 5 minutes, until mixture is thickened.

Each serving (¹/₄ cup) provides: ¹/₄ Fat, 1¹/₂ Vegetables

Per serving: 48 Calories, 2 g Total Fat, 0 g Saturated Fat, 0 mg Cholesterol, 23 mg Sodium, 7 g Total Carbohydrate, 1 g Dietary Fiber, 2 g Protein, 14 mg Calcium

SALSA X-NI-PEK

This strange-looking name means sauce hot enough to heat a dog's nose—and it is! Habanero peppers are more than hot, with a fruity aroma like no other. Removing the seeds and veins will cool the fire a bit. By all means, *wear gloves* when handling this pepper! Serve this sauce as a condiment with just about anything: eggs, fish, poultry or meat, or stir a spoonful into soup just before serving. Recipe may be prepared ahead; refrigerate, covered, for up to 3 days.

Makes 6 servings

1 cup finely chopped yellow
   tomatoes*
1/2 cup minced red onion
1/2 cup loosely packed finely
   chopped fresh cilantro
1 medium habanero pepper,
   seeded, deveined and minced†
   (see page v)

1/2 teaspoon grated orange zest‡
2 tablespoons fresh orange juice
1 tablespoon fresh lime juice
1 tablespoon grapefruit juice

In small bowl, combine tomatoes, onion, cilantro, pepper, zest and orange, lime and grapefruit juices; let stand 30 minutes, until flavors are blended.

Each serving (1/4 cup) provides: 3/4 Vegetable, 5 Optional Calories

Per serving: 17 Calories, 0 g Total Fat, 0 g Saturated Fat, 0 mg Cholesterol, 5 mg Sodium, 4 g Total Carbohydrate, 1 g Dietary Fiber, 1 g Protein, 9 mg Calcium

* *Yellow tomatoes give this sauce a gorgeous color, but if they are not available use red ones.*

† *If habanero peppers are not available, substitute 2 medium serrano peppers.*

‡*The zest of the orange is the peel without any of the pith (white membrane). To remove zest from orange, use a zester or the side of a vegetable grater.*

Tomato-Melon Salsa with Tortilla Chips

Homemade tortilla chips are so much better than the store-bought ones, and they make a great snack. Here, we've teamed them up with a wonderful sweet and savory salsa.

Makes 4 servings

3$^1/_2$ cups chopped tomatoes
1 cup pared and chopped
   cantaloupe or honeydew
   melon
$^1/_2$ cup chopped red onion
$^1/_4$ cup chopped fresh cilantro
2 tablespoons fresh orange juice

2 tablespoons fresh lime juice
1 medium jalapeño pepper,
   seeded, deveined and finely
   chopped (see page v)
Pinch salt
Eight 6" whole-wheat tortillas,
   quartered

1. To prepare salsa, in large bowl combine tomatoes, cantaloupe, onion, cilantro, orange and lime juices, pepper and salt; refrigerate, covered, until chilled.
2. Preheat oven to 375°F. Spray baking sheet with nonstick cooking spray.
3. Arrange tortilla quarters in a single layer on large baking sheet; bake 15 minutes, until golden and crisp. Serve with chilled salsa.

Each serving (1$^1/_4$ cups salsa + 8 tortilla chips) provides: $^1/_4$ Fruit, 2$^1/_4$ Vegetables, 2 Breads, 5 Optional Calories

Per serving with cantaloupe: 192 Calories, 3 g Total Fat, 1 g Saturated Fat, 0 mg Cholesterol, 245 mg Sodium, 37 g Total Carbohydrate, 4 g Dietary Fiber, 6 g Protein, 71 mg Calcium

Per serving with honeydew: 193 Calories, 3 g Total Fat, 1 g Saturated Fat, 0 mg Cholesterol, 245 mg Sodium, 37 g Total Carbohydrate, 4 g Dietary Fiber, 6 g Protein, 69 mg Calcium

CHILES EN ESCABECHE (PICKLED PEPPERS)

Tart, spicy pickled peppers are wonderful as a condiment or relish, or add them to a salad or appetizer platter. Once made, keep refrigerated up to 2 weeks.

Makes 8 servings

8 ounces fresh hot chile peppers
(see page v)
3 medium carrots, cut into
$^1/_8$" slices
$1^1/_2$ teaspoons coarse
(kosher) salt
7 bay leaves
2 large garlic cloves, peeled
$^1/_2$ teaspoon cumin seeds
$^1/_2$ teaspoon dried thyme leaves

$^1/_2$ teaspoon dried oregano leaves
4 whole black peppercorns
2 whole cloves
1 teaspoon corn oil
8 ounces whole baby onions,
halved, or Spanish onion, cut
into $^1/_2$" chunks
1 cup cider vinegar
5 small garlic cloves, peeled
1 teaspoon granulated sugar

1. In large bowl, combine chile peppers, carrots and salt, tossing to combine; let stand 1 hour.
2. In blender, combine 5 bay leaves, the large garlic cloves, cumin, thyme, oregano, peppercorns, whole cloves and $^1/_4$ cup water; purée until smooth.
3. In large nonstick skillet, heat oil; add onions and pureed spice mixture. Cook over medium heat, covered, 3 minutes.
4. Drain chile pepper mixture; reserve liquid. Add chile pepper mixture to onion mixture; cook, covered, 3 minutes longer.
5. Add vinegar, small garlic cloves, sugar, reserved liquid and remaining 2 bay leaves to chile pepper mixture; bring liquid to a boil. Cook over high heat just until carrots are tender-crisp. Remove from heat; let cool.
6. Transfer chile pepper mixture to nonreactive container*; refrigerate, covered, overnight. Drain; remove and discard bay leaves.

Each serving ($^1/_2$ cup) provides: $1^1/_2$ Vegetables, 5 Optional Calories

Per serving: 57 Calories, 0 g Total Fat, 0 g Saturated Fat, 0 mg Cholesterol, 295 mg Sodium, 13 g Total Carbohydrate, 2 g Dietary Fiber, 2 g Protein, 42 mg Calcium

---

* It's best to marinate in containers made of nonreactive material, such as glass, stainless steel or ceramic; ingredients such as vinegar may react with other materials, causing color and flavor changes in foods.

PICKLED ONIONS

Traditionally served with Pollo Pibil (see page 32), these pickled red onions are wonderful with grilled meat and poultry, piled onto a cheese sandwich or tossed into a salad. Once made, they will keep for several weeks in the refrigerator.

Makes 8 servings

2 medium red onions, cut into $^1/_8$" slices	$^1/_2$ teaspoon ground cumin
$^1/_2$ cup cider vinegar	$^1/_2$ teaspoon dried oregano leaves
3 large garlic cloves, lightly crushed	$^1/_2$ teaspoon salt
$^1/_2$ teaspoon coarsely ground black pepper	$^1/_4$ teaspoon ground cloves

1. In medium saucepan, cover onions with cold water. Bring liquid to a boil; cook over high heat 30 seconds. Drain; return onions to saucepan.
2. Add vinegar, garlic, pepper, cumin, oregano, salt, cloves and $^1/_3$ cup water to onions. Bring liquid to a boil; cook over high heat 1 minute. Remove from heat; let cool.
3. Transfer onion mixture to nonreactive container*; refrigerate, covered, overnight. Drain; remove and discard garlic.

Each serving ($^1/_4$ cup) provides: $^1/_4$ Vegetable

Per serving: 11 Calories, 0 g Total Fat, 0 g Saturated Fat, 0 mg Cholesterol, 70 mg Sodium, 3 g Total Carbohydrate, 0 g Dietary Fiber, 0 g Protein, 10 mg Calcium

* *It's best to marinate in containers made of nonreactive material, such as glass, stainless steel or ceramic; ingredients such as vinegar may react with other materials, causing color and flavor changes in foods.*

DESSERTS

Coffee Flan with Chocolate Sauce
Arroz con Leche (Rice Pudding)
Pay de Queso (Cheesecake)
Mexi-Cocoa Cake
Tropical Fruit with Rum Cream
"Fried" Plantain
Cinnamon-Apple Tortilla Cups
Poached Fruit with Rum and Chile Peppers
Frozen Vanilla-Cinnamon Custard
Mexican Chocolate Sherbet
Coconut Sherbet
Margarita Ice
Salsa Sorbet
Chocolate Meringues
Almond-Lime Torte
Coconut-Almond Pie

COFFEE FLAN WITH CHOCOLATE SAUCE

Makes 4 servings

Flan:
1 1/2 cups evaporated skimmed milk
3/4 cup egg substitute
3 tablespoons granulated sugar
1 teaspoon instant coffee powder, dissolved in 1 tablespoon hot water
1/2 teaspoon vanilla extract

Sauce:
1/2 ounce semisweet chocolate, chopped
1 tablespoon boiling water
1 fluid ounce (2 tablespoons) coffee liqueur
Fresh mint leaves, to garnish

1. Preheat oven to 325°F. Adjust oven rack to divide oven in half. Spray 4 custard cups with nonstick cooking spray.*
2. To prepare flan, in medium bowl, combine milk, egg substitute, sugar, dissolved coffee powder and vanilla; divide evenly among prepared cups.
3. Place roasting pan on center oven rack; add filled cups. Carefully pour boiling water into pan to a depth of about 1"; bake 40–45 minutes, until a knife inserted into center of one flan comes out clean.
4. Carefully remove roasting pan from oven and cups from pan; set cups aside to cool. Refrigerate, covered, at least 4 hours.
5. To prepare sauce, in double boiler or small microwave-safe bowl, combine chocolate and boiling water. Set double boiler over barely simmering water; cook 5 minutes, or microwave on High (100% power), 15 seconds. Stir until smooth, then stir in liqueur; set aside.
6. Loosen flans from cups by running tip of pointed knife around edge of each flan. Invert individual dessert plate onto each flan; invert plates and cups together. Remove cups, allowing flans to fall onto plates. Spoon sauce evenly over flans.

Each serving (1 flan + 1 tablespoon sauce) provides: 3/4 Milk, 3/4 Protein, 80 Optional Calories

Per serving: 175 Calories, 1 g Total Fat, 1 g Saturated Fat, 4 mg Cholesterol, 186 mg Sodium, 26 g Total Carbohydrate, 0 g Dietary Fiber, 12 g Protein, 294 mg Calcium

* *If desired, flan can be prepared in 4-cup ovenproof ring mold; increase baking time to 45–55 minutes.*

ARROZ CON LECHE (RICE PUDDING)

This lusciously creamy rice pudding tastes as rich as you'd expect, but because it's made with low-fat ingredients, such as skim milk and egg substitute, you can enjoy it without worry!

Makes 4 servings

4 ounces uncooked regular (not converted) long-grain rice
Two 2 × $^1/_2$" strips lime zest*
One 1" piece cinnamon stick
Pinch salt
2 cups skim milk
$^1/_4$ cup + 1 tablespoon granulated sugar

$^1/_2$ cup egg substitute
2 tablespoons raisins, chopped
1 teaspoon vanilla extract
$^1/_8$ teaspoon ground cinnamon
1 teaspoon stick margarine, melted

1. Spray 1-quart baking dish with nonstick cooking spray.
2. In medium saucepan, combine rice, zest, cinnamon stick, salt and 1$^1/_4$ cups water; bring liquid to a boil. Reduce heat to low; simmer, covered, 20 minutes, until rice is tender and water is absorbed.
3. Add milk and $^1/_4$ cup of the sugar to rice mixture. Increase heat to medium; cook, stirring frequently, 15 minutes. Remove from heat; remove and discard zest and cinnamon stick.
4. Preheat broiler.
5. Add egg substitute, raisins and vanilla to rice mixture. Transfer mixture to prepared baking dish; smooth top.
6. In small bowl, combine ground cinnamon and reserved 1 tablespoon sugar. Brush rice mixture evenly with margarine; sprinkle with cinnamon mixture. Broil 4" from heat, 2–4 minutes, until lightly browned; cool to lukewarm or room temperature.

Each serving ($^3/_4$ cup) provides: $^1/_2$ Milk, $^1/_4$ Fat, $^1/_4$ Fruit, $^1/_2$ Protein, 1 Bread, 55 Optional Calories

Per serving: 167 Calories, 1 g Total Fat, 0 g Saturated Fat, 2 mg Cholesterol, 107 mg Sodium, 33 g Total Carbohydrate, 0 g Dietary Fiber, 6 g Protein, 115 mg Calcium

---

* *The zest of the lime is the peel without any of the pith (white membrane). To remove zest from lime, use a zester or side of a vegetable grater; wrap lime in plastic wrap and refrigerate for use at another time.*

PAY DE QUESO (CHEESECAKE)

Makes 8 servings

Crust:

4 slices firm white bread, diced
1 tablespoon granulated sugar
2 tablespoons fresh lemon juice

$^1/_2$ teaspoon vanilla extract
$^1/_2$ teaspoon almond extract

Filling:

1 pound yogurt cheese*
1 cup nonfat ricotta cheese
$^3/_4$ cup egg substitute
$^1/_4$ cup + 2 tablespoons
   granulated sugar
1 teaspoon vanilla extract

$^1/_4$ teaspoon salt
$^1/_4$ teaspoon ground cinnamon
$^1/_4$ cup golden raisins,
   coarsely chopped
1 tablespoon all-purpose flour

1. Spray 8" springform pan or pie plate with nonstick cooking spray.
2. To prepare crust, in food processor or blender, grind bread into fine crumbs; transfer to small bowl.
3. Add sugar to bread crumbs; stir to combine. Add juice, vanilla and almond extract; toss with a fork until evenly moistened.
4. Press crumb mixture evenly over bottom and up sides of prepared pan; chill.
5. Preheat oven to 375°F. Adjust oven racks to divide oven into thirds.
6. To prepare filling, in clean food processor or blender, combine yogurt and ricotta cheeses, egg substitute, sugar, vanilla, salt and cinnamon; purée until very smooth. Transfer cheese mixture to large bowl.
7. In small bowl, combine raisins and flour; fold into cheese mixture. Pour mixture into prepared crust; bake 5 minutes. Reduce oven temperature to 325°F; bake 40 minutes longer. Turn oven off; let stand in turned-off oven 20 minutes. Remove from oven; cool to room temperature.

Each serving ($^1/_8$ of cake) provides: $^1/_2$ Milk, $^1/_4$ Fruit, $^3/_4$ Protein, $^1/_2$ Bread, 45 Optional Calories

Per serving: 180 Calories, 1 g Total Fat, 0 g Saturated Fat, 3 mg Cholesterol, 243 mg Sodium, 29 g Total Carbohydrate, 1 g Dietary Fiber, 13 g Protein, 325 mg Calcium

* *To prepare yogurt cheese, line a colander with cheesecloth; place in deep bowl. Spoon 1 quart plain nonfat yogurt (without gelatin or other additives) into colander; refrigerate, covered, 1 day. Discard accumulated liquid. Makes about 1 pound.*

MEXI-COCOA CAKE

A pleasantly surprising bite follows the sweetness in this unusual chocolate cake.

Makes 8 servings

$^1/_2$ cup whole-wheat flour

$^1/_2$ cup minus 1 tablespoon all-purpose flour

$^1/_4$ cup + 1 tablespoon firmly packed dark brown sugar

$^1/_4$ cup unsweetened cocoa powder

1 teaspoon double-acting baking powder

$^1/_2$ teaspoon salt

$^1/_4$ teaspoon ground cinnamon

1 cup low-fat (1.5%) buttermilk

1 egg

1 tablespoon + 1 teaspoon corn oil

1 teaspoon pureed canned chipotle peppers in adobo sauce (see page vi for ingredient information)

1 ounce almonds, finely chopped

1. Preheat oven to 375°F. Spray 8" round cake pan with nonstick cooking spray.

2. In medium bowl, combine whole-wheat and all-purpose flours, $^1/_4$ cup of the sugar, and the cocoa, baking powder, salt and cinnamon. In small bowl, with wire whisk, combine buttermilk, egg, oil and peppers. Add wet ingredients to dry, stir just to combine.

3. Transfer batter to prepared cake pan. In small cup, combine almonds and remaining 1 tablespoon sugar; sprinkle evenly over batter. Bake 20 minutes, until toothpick inserted in center of cake comes out clean. Serve warm.

Each serving provides: $^3/_4$ Fat, $^1/_4$ Protein, $^1/_2$ Bread, 60 Optional Calories

Per serving: 154 Calories, 6 g Total Fat, 1 g Saturated Fat, 28 mg Cholesterol, 252 mg Sodium, 23 g Total Carbohydrate, 2 g Dietary Fiber, 5 g Protein, 98 mg Calcium

TROPICAL FRUIT WITH RUM CREAM

This warm, rum-scented sauce served over chilled fruit makes a light but luscious ending to any meal. Be sure to pick the most fragrant and perfect fruit for this pretty dessert.

Makes 8 servings

Fruit:
1 medium papaya, pared, seeded and sliced
1 medium banana, peeled and sliced
1 small mango, pared, pitted and sliced
$^1/_4$ medium pineapple, pared and diced, or 1 cup drained canned pineapple chunks (no sugar added)
$^1/_3$ cup fresh orange juice
2 tablespoons fresh lime juice

Rum Cream:
2 tablespoons firmly packed light brown sugar
2 teaspoons cornstarch
One $2 \times ^1/_2$" strip orange zest*
Pinch ground cinnamon
1 cup evaporated skimmed milk
1 fluid ounce (2 tablespoons) dark rum

1. To prepare fruit, in large bowl, combine papaya, banana, mango, pineapple and orange and lime juices; refrigerate, covered, until chilled.
2. To prepare rum cream, in small saucepan, combine sugar, cornstarch, zest and cinnamon; with wire whisk, stir in milk. Cook over medium heat, stirring constantly with whisk, until mixture comes to a boil. Reduce heat to low; simmer, stirring frequently, 5 minutes, until slightly thickened.
3. Stir rum into milk mixture; remove from heat.
4. With slotted spoon, transfer fruit to serving platter; reserve liquid.
5. Add $^1/_4$ cup reserved liquid to milk mixture; pour remaining juice over fruit. Serve rum cream with fruit.

Each serving ($^3/_4$ cup fruit + 3 tablespoons sauce) provides: $^1/_4$ Milk, 1 Fruit, 30 Optional Calories

Per serving with fresh pineapple: 105 Calories, 0 g Total Fat, 0 g Saturated Fat, 1 mg Cholesterol, 40 mg Sodium, 22 g Total Carbohydrate, 1 g Dietary Fiber, 3 g Protein, 111 mg Calcium

Per serving with canned pineapple: 113 Calories, 0 g Total Fat, 0 g Saturated Fat, 1 mg Cholesterol, 40 mg Sodium, 24 g Total Carbohydrate, 1 g Dietary Fiber, 3 g Protein, 114 mg Calcium

* The zest of the orange is the peel without any of the pith (white membrane). To remove zest from orange, use a zester or side of a vegetable grater; wrap orange in plastic wrap and refrigerate for use at another time.

"FRIED" PLANTAIN

Plantain is an amazing vegetable that, depending on its degree of ripeness, can be served as either a starch or a sweet. Here, it is sweet, served in a rich syrup of rum, margarine and cinnamon, with a tart orange topping for contrast.

Makes 4 servings

Orange Cream:

2 tablespoons nonfat sour cream

2 tablespoons plain nonfat yogurt

$^1/_2$ teaspoon finely grated orange zest*

2 teaspoons fresh orange juice

Plantain:

1 ounce pignolias (pine nuts), slivered almonds or chopped walnuts

2 teaspoons unsalted stick margarine

12 ounces peeled black-ripe plantain, cut into $^1/_4$" slices (see page vii for ingredient information)

2 tablespoons firmly packed dark brown sugar

1 fluid ounce (2 tablespoons) dark rum

$^1/_4$ teaspoon ground cinnamon

1. To prepare orange cream, in small bowl, combine sour cream, yogurt, zest and juice; let stand 30 minutes, until flavors are blended.

2. To prepare plantain, in medium nonstick skillet, toast pignolias over medium-low heat, stirring frequently, until golden brown. Transfer to small bowl; set aside.

3. In same skillet, melt margarine; add plantain. Cook over medium heat 1 minute on each side, until golden brown.

4. Add sugar, rum, cinnamon and $^1/_4$ cup water to plantain mixture; bring liquid to a boil. Reduce heat to low; simmer 5 minutes, until plantain is tender. With slotted spoon, transfer plantain to serving bowl; reserve liquid and set plantain aside.

5. Cook reserved liquid, stirring constantly, 2–3 minutes, until syrupy. Pour syrup over plantain; sprinkle with reserved pignolias. Serve with orange cream.

Each serving (3 ounces plantain, $^1/_4$ of the syrup and nuts +
1 tablespoon cream) provides: 1 Fat, $^1/_4$ Protein, 1 Bread, 55 Optional Calories

Per serving with pignolias: 210 Calories, 6 g Total Fat, 1 g Saturated Fat,
0 mg Cholesterol, 17 mg Sodium, 36 g Total Carbohydrate, 0 g Dietary
Fiber, 4 g Protein, 37 mg Calcium

Per serving with almonds: 215 Calories, 6 g Total Fat, 1 g Saturated Fat,
0 mg Cholesterol, 17 mg Sodium, 37 g Total Carbohydrate, 0 g Dietary
Fiber, 3 g Protein, 54 mg Calcium

Per serving with walnuts: 219 Calories, 7 g Total Fat, 1 g Saturated Fat,
0 mg Cholesterol, 17 mg Sodium, 37 g Total Carbohydrate,
0 g Dietary Fiber, 3 g Protein, 41 mg Calcium

 * *The zest of the orange is the peel without any of the pith (white membrane). To remove zest from orange, use a zester or the side of a vegetable grater.*

VARIATION:

Buttery "Fried" Plantain: Substitute 2 teaspoons sweet butter for the
margarine; reduce Fat Selection to 1/2 and increase Optional Calories
to 70.

Per serving with pignolias: 210 Calories, 6 g Total Fat, 2 g Saturated Fat,
5 mg Cholesterol, 17 mg Sodium, 36 g Total Carbohydrate, 0 g Dietary
Fiber, 4 g Protein, 37 mg Calcium

Per serving with almonds: 215 Calories, 6 g Total Fat, 2 g Saturated Fat,
5 mg Cholesterol, 17 mg Sodium, 37 g Total Carbohydrate, 0 g Dietary
Fiber, 3 g Protein, 54 mg Calcium

Per serving with walnuts: 219 Calories, 7 g Total Fat, 2 g Saturated Fat,
5 mg Cholesterol, 17 mg Sodium, 37 g Total Carbohydrate, 0 g Dietary
Fiber, 3 g Protein, 41 mg Calcium

CINNAMON-APPLE TORTILLA CUPS

This delightful dessert makes wonderful use of the tortilla as a cup for a filling. Try filling the cups with fresh berries in season or any other favorite fruit for a fast and elegant treat.

Makes 4 servings

1 tablespoon + 1 teaspoon
  granulated sugar
1 teaspoon ground cinnamon
Four 6" flour tortillas
4 small baking apples, pared,
  cored and shredded

$^3/_4$ cup plain nonfat yogurt
$^1/_4$ teaspoon ground nutmeg
$^1/_4$ cup whipped topping

1. Preheat oven to 350°F.
2. In small bowl, combine 2 teaspoons of the sugar and $^1/_2$ teaspoon of the cinnamon.
3. Lightly spray both sides of tortillas with nonstick cooking spray; sprinkle both sides evenly with sugar mixture.
4. Press tortillas into 4 muffin or custard cups, forming 4 tortilla cups; bake 5–7 minutes, until edges begin to brown. Remove from oven; place cups on wire rack to cool (if any tortilla cups have become misshapen, reshape while still warm).
5. In medium bowl, combine apples, yogurt, nutmeg, remaining 2 teaspoons sugar and remaining $^1/_2$ teaspoon cinnamon; refrigerate, covered, until chilled.
6. Remove tortilla cups from muffin cups; fill each with an equal amount of apple mixture. Top each portion with 1 tablespoon whipped topping; serve immediately.

Each serving (1 filled tortilla cup) provides: $^1/_4$ Milk, 1 Fruit, 1 Bread, 30 Optional Calories

Per serving: 182 Calories, 4 g Total Fat, 1 g Saturated Fat, 1 mg Cholesterol, 128 mg Sodium, 34 g Total Carbohydrate, 2 g Dietary Fiber, 4 g Protein, 121 mg Calcium

POACHED FRUIT WITH RUM AND CHILE PEPPERS

Sweet, then hot, this combination is delicious on its own, with a scoop of Frozen Vanilla-Cinnamon Custard (see page 180) or chilled and served as a relish with cold poultry and pork.

Makes 8 servings

6 ounces mixed dried fruit, diced	One 2" piece cinnamon stick
1 cup apple cider	One 4 × ¹/₂" strip orange zest,*
1 medium fresh hot chile pepper,	studded with 2 whole cloves
seeded and deveined	1 fluid ounce (2 tablespoons)
(see page v)	dark rum

1. In small saucepan, combine dried fruit, cider, pepper, cinnamon stick and zest; bring liquid to a boil. Reduce heat to low; simmer, covered, 10 minutes. Remove from heat; stir in rum. Let stand 1 hour, until flavors are blended.
2. With slotted spoon, divide fruit evenly among 8 dessert dishes; remove and discard pepper, cinnamon stick and zest. Divide liquid evenly over fruit; serve warm.

Each serving (¹/₂ cup) provides: 1¹/₄ Fruits; 10 Optional Calories

Per serving: 76 Calories, 0 g Total Fat, 0 g Saturated Fat, 0 mg Cholesterol, 5 mg Sodium, 18 g Total Carbohydrate, 1 g Dietary Fiber, 1 g Protein, 12 mg Calcium

* The zest of the orange is the peel without any of the pith (white membrane). To remove zest from orange, use a zester or side of a vegetable grater; wrap orange in plastic wrap and refrigerate for use at another time.

VARIATION:

Poached Fruit with Chile Pepper: Substitute cider vinegar for the rum; omit Optional Calories.

Per serving: 69 Calories, 0 g Total Fat, 0 g Saturated Fat, 0 mg Cholesterol, 5 mg Sodium, 18 g Total Carbohydrate, 1 g Dietary Fiber, 1 g Protein, 12 mg Calcium

Frozen Vanilla-Cinnamon Custard

Serve this rich frozen dessert as the finish to an elegant meal. Top it with Poached Fruit with Rum and Chile Peppers (see page 179) or some pureed fresh mango if you like, or make the ultimate dessert sandwich by freezing it in a 9" square pan, cutting it into squares and placing it between graham crackers.

Makes 4 servings

$^{1}/_{2}$ cup skim milk	1 cup evaporated skimmed milk
$^{1}/_{4}$ cup granulated sugar	$^{1}/_{2}$ cup egg substitute
One 2" piece cinnamon stick	$1^{1}/_{2}$ teaspoons vanilla extract
or $^{1}/_{4}$ teaspoon ground	1 drop yellow food coloring
cinnamon	(optional)

1. In small saucepan, combine skim milk, sugar and cinnamon; cook over low heat, stirring frequently, 10 minutes. Remove from heat; let stand 30 minutes, until flavors are blended.
2. Transfer milk mixture to medium bowl; add evaporated skimmed milk, egg substitute, vanilla and food coloring if using. Refrigerate, covered, until chilled.
3. Remove and discard cinnamon stick from milk mixture if using. Transfer mixture to ice-cream maker; freeze, following manufacturer's directions.
4. Transfer frozen mixture to 1-quart freezer-safe container; freeze at least 2 hours longer.

Each serving ($^{1}/_{2}$ cup) provides: $^{1}/_{2}$ Milk, $^{1}/_{2}$ Protein, 55 Optional Calories

Per serving: 130 Calories, 0 g Total Fat, 0 g Saturated Fat, 3 mg Cholesterol, 139 mg Sodium, 22 g Total Carbohydrate, 0 g Dietary Fiber, 9 g Protein, 235 mg Calcium

Variation:

Frozen Vanilla-Rum Custard: Add 1 fluid ounce (2 tablespoons) dark rum along with evaporated skimmed milk; increase Optional Calories to 75.

Per serving: 146 Calories, 0 g Total Fat, 0 g Saturated Fat, 3 mg Cholesterol, 139 mg Sodium, 22 g Total Carbohydrate, 0 g Dietary Fiber, 9 g Protein, 235 mg Calcium

MEXICAN CHOCOLATE SHERBET

Not technically authentic but so simply delicious, this subtle chocolate iced treat makes a spectacular finish to a special dinner. If you do not have an ice-cream maker, freeze it in a shallow dish, beating with an electric mixer several times to keep it smooth. Serve it in your prettiest dishes, garnished with cinnamon sticks.

Makes 6 servings

$^1/_4$ cup + 2 tablespoons
granulated sugar
$^1/_4$ cup + 2 tablespoons
unsweetened cocoa powder
$1^1/_2$ cups boiling water
Zest of 1 small orange*
One $1^1/_2$" piece cinnamon stick

2 cups skim milk
$1^1/_2$ cups evaporated skimmed
milk
$^1/_2$ teaspoon almond extract
Additional cinnamon sticks, to
garnish

1. In medium saucepan, with wire whisk, combine sugar, cocoa and boiling water, blending until smooth. Add zest and cinnamon stick; bring liquid to a boil. Reduce heat to low; simmer, stirring frequently, 10 minutes.
2. Add skim and evaporated skimmed milks and almond extract to sugar mixture; remove from heat. Refrigerate, covered, until chilled.
3. Remove and discard zest and cinnamon stick from milk mixture. Transfer mixture to ice-cream maker; freeze, following manufacturer's directions.
4. Transfer frozen mixture to $1^1/_2$-quart freezer-safe container; freeze at least 1 hour longer. Serve garnished with cinnamon sticks.

Each serving ($^3/_4$ cup) provides: $^3/_4$ Milk, 70 Optional Calories

Per serving: 141 Calories, 1 g Total Fat, 1 g Saturated Fat, 4 mg Cholesterol, 117 mg Sodium, 27 g Total Carbohydrate, 2 g Dietary Fiber, 9 g Protein, 295 mg Calcium

* The zest of the orange is the peel without any of the pith (white membrane). To remove zest from orange, use a zester or side of a vegetable grater; wrap orange in plastic wrap and refrigerate for use at another time.

COCONUT SHERBET

Rich yet refreshing, this sherbet makes a lovely finish to a gala dinner, or enjoy it as a cooling summer snack.

Makes 4 servings

1 cup skim milk	$^1/_4$ teaspoon coconut oil
$^1/_4$ cup granulated sugar	$^1/_4$ teaspoon vanilla extract
1 cup evaporated skimmed milk	$^1/_2$ cup shredded coconut

1. In small saucepan, combine skim milk and sugar; cook over low heat, stirring constantly, until sugar is dissolved. Add evaporated skimmed milk, coconut oil and vanilla; refrigerate, covered, until chilled.
2. Transfer mixture to ice-cream maker; freeze, following manufacturer's directions.
3. Transfer frozen mixture to 1-quart freezer-safe container; freeze at least 2 hours longer.
4. Preheat oven to 325°F.
5. Spread coconut in small pie plate; bake, stirring once or twice, 5 minutes, until golden brown. Cool; sprinkle each serving of sherbet with 1 tablespoon coconut.

Each serving ($^1/_2$ cup sherbet + 1 tablespoon coconut) provides:
3/4 Milk, 65 Optional Calories

Per serving: 145 Calories, 2 g Total Fat, 2 g Saturated Fat, 4 mg Cholesterol, 117 mg Sodium, 25 g Total Carbohydrate, 0 g Dietary Fiber, 7 g Protein, 261 mg Calcium

MARGARITA ICE

Less alcoholic than a frozen margarita, this spiked fruit ice makes a refreshing, tart finish to a rich meal. You will get more juice out of the limes if you warm them in a bowl of hot water or the microwave before squeezing. If you don't have an ice-cream maker, freeze mixture in a shallow freezer-safe container until slushy; beat until smooth. Freeze and beat again, until mixture is firm. Beat again just before serving.

Makes 4 servings

Zest of 3 limes*
$^1/_4$ cup + 1 tablespoon granulated sugar

$^3/_4$ cup fresh lime juice
$1^1/_2$ fluid ounces (3 tablespoons) tequila

1. In small saucepan, combine zest, sugar and $^3/_4$ cup water; bring liquid to a boil. Reduce heat to low; simmer, covered, 10 minutes. Remove from heat; let stand 1 hour, until flavors are blended.
2. With slotted spoon, remove and discard zest; transfer liquid to medium bowl. Add juice and tequila; stir to combine.
3. Transfer mixture to ice-cream maker; freeze, following manufacturer's directions.
4. Transfer frozen mixture to 1-quart freezer-safe container; freeze at least 1 hour longer.

Each serving ($^1/_2$ cup) provides: 85 Optional Calories

Per serving: 100 Calories, 0 g Total Fat, 0 g Saturated Fat, 0 mg Cholesterol, 1 mg Sodium, 20 g Total Carbohydrate, 0 g Dietary Fiber, 0 g Protein, 6 mg Calcium

* *The zest of the lime is the peel without any of the pith (white membrane). To remove zest from lime, use a zester or side of a vegetable grater.*

Salsa Sorbet

Make this when tomatoes are in season, using the most fragrant ones you can find—or grow. For a fabulous, and unexpected, color, try it with yellow tomatoes. Serve this refreshing ice as an unexpected first course, between courses as a palate refresher or as a cooling treat on a hot day.

Makes 8 servings

8 medium tomatoes, quartered
1 medium jalapeño pepper, seeded, deveined and coarsely chopped (see page v)
¹/₄ cup chopped onion
6 fresh cilantro sprigs
1 tablespoon fresh lime juice
1 teaspoon granulated sugar
1 small clove garlic, peeled
¹/₄ teaspoon salt
Lime slices and additional fresh cilantro sprigs, to garnish

1. In food processor or blender, combine tomatoes, pepper, onion, cilantro, juice, sugar, garlic and salt; purée until very smooth.
2. Place medium sieve over medium bowl. Strain tomato mixture through sieve, pressing with back of wooden spoon; discard solids. Refrigerate, covered, until chilled.
3. Transfer mixture to ice-cream maker; freeze, following manufacturer's directions. Serve garnished with lime slices and cilantro sprigs.

Each serving (¹/₂ cup) provides: 2¹/₄ Vegetables

Per serving: 38 Calories, 1 g Total Fat, 0 g Saturated Fat, 0 mg Cholesterol, 82 mg Sodium, 9 g Total Carbohydrate, 2 g Dietary Fiber, 1 g Protein, 11 mg Calcium

VARIATION:

Mexican Mary: Add 1 fluid ounce (2 tablespoons) tequila or gin before freezing; add 10 Optional Calories to Selection Information.

Per serving: 47 Calories, 1 g Total Fat, 0 g Saturated Fat, 0 mg Cholesterol, 82 mg Sodium, 9 g Total Carbohydrate, 2 g Dietary Fiber, 1 g Protein, 11 mg Calcium

CHOCOLATE MERINGUES

Intensely chocolatey, these little confections are delicious with a foamy cup of Café de Olla (see page 195) or tea.

Makes 28 servings

3 egg whites, at room temperature
Pinch cream of tartar
Pinch salt
$^{1}/_{2}$ cup granulated sugar
$^{1}/_{2}$ teaspoon vanilla extract
$^{1}/_{2}$ teaspoon almond extract

2 ounces blanched almonds, ground
2 tablespoons + 1 teaspoon unsweetened cocoa powder
$^{1}/_{2}$ teaspoon ground cinnamon

1. Preheat oven to 275°F. Spray baking sheet with nonstick cooking spray.
2. In medium bowl, combine egg whites, cream of tartar and salt; with electric mixer on high speed, beat mixture until soft peaks form. Set aside.
3. In small saucepan, combine sugar and $^{1}/_{4}$ cup water; bring liquid to a boil. Reduce heat to medium; cook, covered, 30 seconds. Remove cover; cook 2–3 minutes longer, until soft ball stage (238°F on candy thermometer).
4. With electric mixer on high speed, slowly pour sugar mixture into egg white mixture; continue beating until mixture is stiff and glossy. Beat in vanilla and almond extracts.
5. In small bowl, combine almonds, 2 tablespoons of the cocoa and the cinnamon; fold into egg white mixture.
6. Drop egg white mixture by heaping teaspoonsful onto prepared baking sheet, making 28 meringues; bake 1$^{1}/_{2}$ hours, until outsides of meringues are firm.
7. With spatula, transfer meringues to wire rack. Sift remaining 1 teaspoon cocoa through fine sieve over meringues; let cool.

Each serving (1 meringue) provides: 25 Optional Calories

Per serving: 29 Calories, 1 g Total Fat, 0 g Saturated Fat, 0 mg Cholesterol, 11 mg Sodium, 4 g Total Carbohydrate, 0 g Dietary Fiber, 1 g Protein, 6 mg Calcium

ALMOND-LIME TORTE

A not-too-sweet cake that goes beautifully with afternoon coffee or tea, as well as after dinner, this features the characteristic Mexican flavors of lime and almond.

Makes 8 servings

¹/₄ cup granulated sugar
Zest of 1 lime*
6 graham crackers
  (2¹/₄" squares), broken into
  bite-size pieces
2 ounces blanched almonds
2 teaspoons unsalted stick
  margarine, melted

2 egg whites, at room temperature
Pinch cream of tartar
³/₄ cup egg substitute
¹/₂ teaspoon almond extract
1 teaspoon confectioners sugar

1. Preheat oven to 350°F. Adjust oven rack to divide oven in half. Spray 8" springform pan with nonstick cooking spray.
2. In food processor or blender, combine granulated sugar and zest; process until finely ground. Transfer sugar mixture to small plate; set aside.
3. In food processor containing sugar mixture residue, combine graham crackers and almonds; process until finely crumbled (do not let mixture become too powdery). Transfer crumb mixture to small bowl. Add margarine; toss to moisten evenly. Set aside.
4. In medium bowl, combine egg whites and cream of tartar; with electric mixer on high speed, beat until stiff but not dry. Set aside.
5. In separate medium bowl, combine egg substitute and almond extract; with electric mixer on medium speed, beat, adding reserved sugar mixture 1 tablespoon at a time, 5 minutes, until fluffy. Fold in reserved crumb mixture.
6. Fold egg white mixture into egg substitute mixture; transfer to prepared pan. Bake 25–30 minutes, until toothpick inserted in center comes out clean. Transfer torte to wire rack; let stand 10 minutes. Strain confectioners sugar through small sieve over torte; let cool completely.

Each serving (¹/₈ of cake) provides: ³/₄ Fat, ¹/₂ Protein, ¹/₄ Bread,
  35 Optional Calories

Per serving: 115 Calories, 5 g Total Fat, 1 g Saturated Fat, 0 mg
    Cholesterol, 84 mg Sodium, 12 g Total Carbohydrate, 1 g Dietary Fiber,
    5 g Protein, 28 mg Calcium

* *The zest of the lime is the peel without any of the pith (white membrane). To remove zest from lime, use a zester or side of a vegetable grater; wrap lime in plastic wrap and refrigerate for use at another time.*

VARIATION:

Buttery Almond-Lime Torte: Substitute 2 teaspoons sweet butter, melted,
    for the margarine; reduce Fat Selection to 1/2 and increase Optional
    Calories to 45.

Per serving: 115 Calories, 5 g Total Fat, 1 g Saturated Fat, 3 mg Choles-
    terol, 84 mg Sodium, 12 g Total Carbohydrate, 1 g Dietary Fiber,
    5 g Protein, 28 mg Calcium

COCONUT-ALMOND PIE

Crustless, with a crunchy topping, this creamy pie is a masterful finale to a special meal.

Makes 8 servings

6 graham crackers
(2¹/₂" squares), finely crushed
¹/₂ cup shredded coconut
¹/₂ ounce sliced almonds
2 cups evaporated skimmed milk
1 cup egg substitute

¹/₄ cup granulated sugar
1 teaspoon coconut oil
1 teaspoon vanilla extract
¹/₂ teaspoon almond extract
¹/₄ teaspoon ground cinnamon

1. Preheat oven to 325°F. Adjust oven rack to divide oven in half. Spray a deep, 9" glass or ceramic pie plate or 8" springform pan with nonstick cooking spray.
2. Sprinkle bottom of pie plate or sides of springform pan with 2 tablespoons of the graham cracker crumbs; set aside.
3. Spread coconut and almonds evenly in small baking pan; bake, stirring once or twice, 5 minutes, until golden brown. Cool; stir in remaining graham cracker crumbs. Set aside.
4. In medium bowl, with wire whisk, combine milk, egg substitute, sugar, oil, vanilla, almond extract and cinnamon. Transfer milk mixture to prepared pie plate; sprinkle evenly with reserved coconut mixture. Bake 35–45 minutes, until knife inserted near center comes out clean. (If topping is getting too brown while baking, cover loosely with foil.) Transfer pie to wire rack to cool.

Each serving (¹/₈ of pie) provides: ¹/₂ Milk, ¹/₂ Protein, ¹/₄ Bread, 50 Optional Calories

Per serving: 152 Calories, 4 g Total Fat, 2 g Saturated Fat, 3 mg Cholesterol, 167 mg Sodium, 21 g Total Carbohydrate, 1 g Dietary Fiber, 9 g Protein, 203 mg Calcium

BEVERAGES

Horchata
Toritos (Limeade)
Licuado with Milk
Licuado with Water
Mexican Hot Chocolate
Café de Olla

HORCHATA

The name may sound peculiar to our modern ears, but this drink is similar to many medieval nonalcoholic beverages. Served very cold, it is wonderfully refreshing.

Makes 6 servings

6 ounces uncooked regular (not converted) long-grain rice
Zest of 1 lime*
5 cups boiling water
¹/₂ cup granulated sugar

1 teaspoon almond extract
¹/₄ teaspoon ground cinnamon
1 cup cold water
Twisted strips of lime zest, to garnish*

1. In blender, combine rice and zest of 1 lime; process until very fine. With blender off, add 2 cups of the boiling water; transfer mixture to 2-quart heatproof container, scraping blender jar with rubber spatula to remove all of mixture.
2. Add remaining 3 cups boiling water, the sugar, almond extract and cinnamon; stir to combine. Cool to room temperature; refrigerate, covered, overnight.
3. Line medium sieve with 3 layers of cheesecloth; place over medium bowl. Strain rice mixture through sieve, squeezing cheesecloth to extract as much liquid as possible; discard solids. Stir cold water into liquid; refrigerate, covered, until chilled. Stir before serving; serve garnished with zest.

Each serving (³/₄ cup) provides: 140 Optional Calories

Per serving: 119 Calories, 0 g Total Fat, 0 g Saturated Fat, 0 mg Cholesterol, 1 mg Sodium, 28 g Total Carbohydrate, 0 g Dietary Fiber, 1 g Protein, 6 mg Calcium

* *The zest of the lime is the peel without any of the pith (white membrane). To remove zest from lime, use a zester or side of a vegetable grater; wrap lime in plastic wrap and refrigerate for use at another time.*

TORITOS (LIMEADE)

This tart, cooling drink has a pleasant undertone of bitterness from the lime zest; it is good just as it is, or with a little tequila or rum added.

Makes 4 servings

¹/₄ cup + 2 tablespoons granulated sugar	1 cup fresh lime juice
Zest of 1 lime*	2 cups seltzer
	Lime slices, to garnish

1. In small saucepan, combine sugar, zest and 1 cup water; bring liquid to a boil. Reduce heat to low; simmer 10 minutes. Remove from heat; let stand 30 minutes, until flavors are blended.
2. Remove and discard zest from sugar mixture; transfer to chilled pitcher. Add juice; stir to combine. Refrigerate, covered, until chilled.
3. Fill 4 tall glasses with ice. Add seltzer to lime mixture; divide among ice-filled glasses. Serve garnished with lime slices.

Each serving (1 cup) provides: 70 Optional Calories

Per serving: 89 Calories, 0 g Total Fat, 0 g Saturated Fat, 0 mg Cholesterol, 1 mg Sodium, 24 g Total Carbohydrate, 0 g Dietary Fiber, 0 g Protein, 6 mg Calcium

* The zest of the lime is the peel without any of the pith (white membrane). To remove zest from lime, use a zester or side of a vegetable grater.

LICUADO WITH MILK

In every little town in Mexico, you will find juice stands with a breathtaking display of tropical fruits that fill the air with their ripe perfumes. If you can find guanabanas or guavas, by all means use them in this recipe, but nectarines, peaches and strawberries are good choices, too. If you choose intensely fragrant fruit, you will need little or no added sugar.

Makes 4 servings

1¹/₂ medium papayas, pared, seeded and cut into chunks; or

1¹/₂ small mangoes, pared, pitted and cut into chunks; or

³/₄ small cantaloupe, pared, seeded and cut into chunks; or

1¹/₂ medium bananas, peeled and cut into chunks

2 cups very cold or slightly frozen skim milk

1 tablespoon granulated sugar

2 teaspoons fresh lime juice

In blender, combine fruit, milk, sugar and juice; purée until smooth. Serve immediately.

Each serving provides: ¹/₂ Milk, ³/₄ Fruit, 10 Optional Calories

Per serving with papaya: 100 Calories, 0 g Total Fat, 0 g Saturated Fat, 2 mg Cholesterol, 67 mg Sodium, 20 g Total Carbohydrate, 1 g Dietary Fiber, 5 g Protein, 178 mg Calcium

Per serving with mangoes: 92 Calories, 0 g Total Fat, 0 g Saturated Fat, 2 mg Cholesterol, 65 mg Sodium, 19 g Total Carbohydrate, 1 g Dietary Fiber, 4 g Protein, 157 mg Calcium

Per serving with cantaloupe: 85 Calories, 0 g Total Fat, 0 g Saturated Fat, 2 mg Cholesterol, 71 mg Sodium, 16 g Total Carbohydrate, 1 g Dietary Fiber, 5 g Protein, 160 mg Calcium

Per serving with bananas: 124 Calories, 0 g Total Fat, 0 g Saturated Fat, 2 mg Cholesterol, 64 mg Sodium, 26 g Total Carbohydrate, 1 g Dietary Fiber, 5 g Protein, 155 mg Calcium

LICUADO WITH WATER

With or without liquor, this smooth, icy drink is the perfect cooler on a scorching summer day. Experiment with different fruits, especially the more juicy ones, such as berries and melons. Be sure the fruit is ripe and fragrant and you won't need to add a drop of sugar.

Makes 4 servings

4 cups strawberries, diced
1 cup ice water
2 tablespoons fresh lime juice
1 fluid ounce (2 tablespoons) rum
   or tequila (optional)

Fresh mint leaves or lime slices, to
   garnish

1. In food processor or blender, purée strawberries until very smooth.
2. Transfer pureed strawberries to freezer-safe pitcher. Add ice water, juice and rum if using; freeze 30 minutes.
3. With wire whisk, blend strawberry mixture until smooth; serve immediately, garnished with mint leaves or lime slices.

Each serving without liquor provides: 1 Fruit

Per serving: 48 Calories, 1 g Total Fat, 0 g Saturated Fat, 0 mg Cholesterol, 2 mg Sodium, 11 g Total Carbohydrate, 4 g Dietary Fiber, 1 g Protein, 22 mg Calcium

Each serving with liquor provides: 1 Fruit, 20 Optional Calories

Per serving with rum: 64 Calories, 1 g Total Fat, 0 g Saturated Fat, 0 mg Cholesterol, 2 mg Sodium, 11 g Total Carbohydrate, 4 g Dietary Fiber, 1 g Protein, 21 mg Calcium

Per serving with tequila: 65 Calories, 1 g Total Fat, 0 g Saturated Fat, 0 mg Cholesterol, 2 mg Sodium, 11 g Total Carbohydrate, 4 g Dietary Fiber, 1 g Protein, 22 mg Calcium

MEXICAN HOT CHOCOLATE

Use this rich, thick chocolate as a dessert or as a hearty snack on a cold day. To help warm you down to your bones, add a splash of coffee or almond liqueur if you like.

Makes 6 servings

¹/4 cup granulated sugar
Zest of 1 small orange*
One 1" piece cinnamon stick
¹/4 cup + 2 tablespoons
  unsweetened cocoa powder

2 tablespoons cornstarch
2 cups skim milk
1¹/2 cups evaporated skimmed milk
¹/2 teaspoon almond extract

1. In large saucepan, combine sugar, zest, cinnamon stick and 1¹/2 cups water; bring liquid to a boil. Reduce heat to low; simmer 20 minutes.
2. In medium bowl, combine cocoa and cornstarch; with wire whisk, add skim and evaporated skimmed milks, blending until cocoa and cornstarch are dissolved.
3. Stir milk mixture into sugar mixture; stirring constantly, bring just to a boil over medium heat. Reduce heat to low; simmer, stirring frequently, 15 minutes. Remove from heat; stir in almond extract. Strain milk mixture into 6 mugs; serve immediately.

Each serving (³/4 cup) provides: ³/4 Milk, 65 Optional Calories

Per serving: 135 Calories, 1 g Total Fat, 1 g Saturated Fat, 4 mg Cholesterol, 117 mg Sodium, 25 g Total Carbohydrate, 2 g Dietary Fiber, 9 g Protein, 294 mg Calcium

* *The zest of the orange is the peel without any of the pith (white membrane). To remove zest from orange, use a zester or side of a vegetable grater; wrap orange in plastic wrap and refrigerate for use at another time.*

CAFÉ DE OLLA

This is so rich tasting that it would make a fine dessert! Make it extra strong and serve it iced in summer. Or you can freeze a batch in ice-cube trays and whirl in a blender for a coffee slush.

Makes 4 servings

$^{1}/_{4}$ cup firmly packed dark brown sugar
Two 2" pieces cinnamon stick or $^{1}/_{2}$ teaspoon ground cinnamon
Zest of $^{1}/_{2}$ small orange*

$^{1}/_{4}$ teaspoon aniseed, crushed
$^{2}/_{3}$ cup Vienna-roast or other light-roast ground coffee grinds (medium grind)

1. In medium saucepan, combine sugar, cinnamon, zest, aniseed and 1 quart water; bring liquid to a boil. Reduce heat to low; simmer, covered, 10 minutes. Remove from heat.
2. Add ground coffee grinds to sugar mixture; stir to combine. Let stand, covered, 5 minutes, until flavors are blended.
3. Stir coffee mixture, then strain into heated coffee pot or 4 coffee mugs.

Each serving (1 cup) provides: 45 Optional Calories

Per serving: 66 Calories, 0 g Total Fat, 0 g Saturated Fat, 0 mg Cholesterol, 17 mg Sodium, 16 g Total Carbohydrate, 0 g Dietary Fiber, 1 g Protein, 30 mg Calcium

The zest of the orange is the peel without any of the pith (white membrane). To remove zest from orange, use a zester or side of a vegetable grater; wrap orange in plastic wrap and refrigerate for use at another time.

Variation:

Café de Olla con Leche: Add 2 cups boiling skim milk to hot coffee just before serving; add $^{1}/_{2}$ Milk Selection to Selection Information.

Per serving: 109 Calories, 0 g Total Fat, 0 g Saturated Fat, 2 mg Cholesterol, 81 mg Sodium, 22 g Total Carbohydrate, 0 g Dietary Fiber, 5 g Protein, 181 mg Calcium

METRIC CONVERSIONS

If you are converting the recipes in this book to
metric measurements, use the following chart as a guide.

Volume		Weight		Length		Oven Temperatures	
¹/₄ teaspoon	1 milliliter	1 ounce	30 grams	1 inch	25 millimeters	250°F	120°C
¹/₂ teaspoon	2 milliliters	¹/₄ pound	120 grams	1 inch	2.5 centimeters	275°F	140°C
1 teaspoon	5 milliliters	¹/₂ pound	240 grams			300°F	150°C
1 tablespoon	15 milliliters	³/₄ pound	360 grams			325°F	160°C
2 tablespoons	30 milliliters	1 pound	480 grams			350°F	180°C
3 tablespoons	45 milliliters					375°F	190°C
¹/₄ cup	50 milliliters					400°F	200°C
¹/₃ cup	75 milliliters					425°F	220°C
¹/₂ cup	125 milliliters					450°F	230°C
²/₃ cup	150 milliliters					475°F	250°C
³/₄ cup	175 milliliters					500°F	260°C
1 cup	250 milliliters					525°F	270°C
1 quart	1 liter						

DRY AND LIQUID MEASUREMENT EQUIVALENTS

Teaspoons	Tablespoons	Cups	Fluid Ounces
3 teaspoons	1 tablespoon		¹/₂ fluid ounce
6 teaspoons	2 tablespoons	¹/₈ cup	1 fluid ounce
8 teaspoons	2 tablespoons plus 2 teaspoons	¹/₆ cup	
12 teaspoons	4 tablespoons	¹/₄ cup	2 fluid ounces
15 teaspoons	5 tablespoons	¹/₃ cup minus 1 teaspoon	
16 teaspoons	5 tablespoons plus 1 teaspoon	¹/₃ cup	
18 teaspoons	6 tablespoons	¹/₃ cup plus two teaspoons	3 fluid ounces
24 teaspoons	8 tablespoons	¹/₂ cup	4 fluid ounces
30 teaspoons	10 tablespoons	¹/₂ cup plus 2 tablespoons	5 fluid ounces
32 teaspoons	10 tablespoons plus 2 teaspoons	²/₃ cup	
36 teaspoons	12 tablespoons	³/₄ cup	6 fluid ounces
42 teaspoons	14 tablespoons	1 cup plus 2 tablespoons	7 fluid ounces
45 teaspoons	15 tablespoons	1 cup minus 1 tablespoon	
48 teaspoons	16 tablespoons	1 cup	8 fluid ounces

Note: Measurement of less than ¹/₈ teaspoon is considered a dash or a pinch.

INDEX